# POSITIVE

# POWER

# POSITIVE POWER

**BARBARA ANN WILLIAMS**

All rights reserved. No part of this book may be reproduced or transmitted in any form or by any means, electronic or mechanical, including photocopying, recording, or by any information storage and retrieval system, without permission in writing from the author.

Barbara Williams

Copyright © 2014 by Barbara Williams

ISBN-13: 978-0984724789
ISBN-10: 0984724788

First Printing 2014
Printed in the United States of America

Cover Photo: Skating coach Barbara Williams with Jack Pensa, Jaime Rapp, Oliver Rapp, and Charles Sikorski.

# DEDICATION

**To my three beautiful children—My two sons, Randy and Tommy Giresi, and my daughter Cyndee Giresi.**
I love you all very much. You are my inspiration in life and for writing all of my books. You are all my "rock."

**To my family—I cherish each and every one of you.**
My sisters: Patricia Grabowski and Michelle Williams. My brothers Andrew and Brian Williams. My brothers-in-law, Steve Grabowski and Tom De Guissippee. My sister-in-law Margo Williams. My nieces and nephews, Justine Graham and Katie Rose Graham, Frankie Capolino and Chris Capolino, Mark Grabowski, Anthony Salerno, Karen Kerns, Debbie Kalinyak, Krystle and Josh Cree, Craig Kalinyak, and Michael, Teri, and Elizabeta Riemenschneider.

**To my beautiful and compassionate sister—Maureen Riemenschneider and her husband Dick who are in heaven, along with my parents Andrew and Christina Williams.**
Not a day goes by that I don't think of all of you. Till we meet again!

                                                          I love you,
                                                          Barbara
                                                          Kings Park, NY
                                                          January 2014

# SPECIAL THANKS

The Ioveno Family:
Joseph, Patty, Anthony, Michael, and Kevin.

Without your help, Joe, I never could have written this book. Thank you for all the countless hours on the computer, scanning all the pictures and typing all the text. You have no idea how much I truly appreciate you helping me with my book. But remember, you are a "layman" to power skating, and I am the "professional." Thanks again for all your work on the goalie chapter.

Thank you, Patty, for all the typing. Michael and Kevin, thank you for your time filming the goalie chapter. Thank you, Anthony for being positive and uplifting to me.

The Barbeisch Family

Thank you, Charlie, for taking over 1,000 pictures for my book. The pictures came out perfect and showed the drills very clearly. Thank you, Diane, for all your help and positive thoughts for me. Thank you for making sure all the pictures were on the computer. You both did a magnificent job and made my book a reality.

Vincent Bivona

What can I say, Vinny? Without your support and encouragement, there would be no book. I can't thank you enough for your guidance and perseverance in telling me to write my book. I'm very happy that I listened to you. You are one in a million, and an unbelievable fellow author.

### In Memoriam

Our photographer's beautiful wife, Diane Barbeisch, passed away during the writing of this book. She will be truly missed. She always was kind and had a good attitude about life. She also encouraged me to write this book. Thank you, Diane, and God bless you.

*January 1977*

Barbara Williams was highly skilled as a power skating coach. She was extremely dependable and always displayed a high degree of integrity, responsibility, and ambition. She had the respect and admiration from all of the New York Islanders, and that is why I named her the *First Female Skating Coach in the National Hockey League*. Her years with the Islanders were positive, especially winning the Stanley Cup in 1980.

**—Al Arbour, Four Stanley Cup champion coach.**

# TABLE OF CONTENTS

**Introduction** ………………………………………………………………………………..11

**Chapter 1: About Barbara Williams** …………………………………………….13

**Chapter 2: Getting In Shape** ……………………………………………………….31

**Chapter 3: Everything You Wanted To Know About Skates** ………………67

**Chapter 4: Power Skating Drills** …………………………………………………..81

**Chapter 5: Balance And Agility** …………………………………………………..105

**Chapter 6: Warm-Ups** ………………………………………………………………115

**Chapter 7: Power Skating For Goaltenders** …………………………………..119

**Chapter 8: Girls Hockey** ……………………………………………………………147

**Chapter 9: Flat Stanley Project** …………………………………………………..155

**Chapter 10: Barbara's Personal Thoughts** ……………………………………..157

**Chapter 11: Bullying** ………………………………………………………………...159

**Chapter 12: Professional Insights** ……………………………………………….161

**Chapter 13: My Students** ………………………………………………………….165

**Acknowledgements** …………………………………………………………………177

# INTRODUCTION

The year is 2014, and I have been a power skating coach for over 30 years. I feel that I am an expert in my field.

My professional background speaks for itself: the First Female Skating Coach in the National Hockey League and the First Woman to Coach a Men's Team on a National Level (named that by the New York Islanders). I was also the official skating coach to the NHL New Jersey Devils, as well as four NHL Farm Teams. In addition to this, I have coached hundreds of NHL pros privately. I have had my own hockey school for over 25 years on Long Island, New York, and I published my first book *More Power to Your Skating* with Macmillan Publishers. This is my second "how to" book on power skating. I named it *Positive Power* because I have always preached positive thinking my entire life. When I was very young, I read the book *The Power of Positive Thinking* by Dr. Norman Vincent Peale. It influenced my entire life and everything that I think, do, and say. I recommend the book or CD for everyone, including parents. It will not only help hockey players with their game, but it will also make a difference in their lives. I live and breathe that book every day!

I am sure many parents and young hockey players have purchased books and CDs on power skating. Most of these are too advanced for the average player and boring as well. My book is simple and direct and will help any hockey player become a better skater. My drills are not complicated, and they are easy to perform. Not only will a player's skating improve, but his or her game will improve as well.

I believe in the sayings "practice makes perfect" and "repetition is the mother of all skill." Practice the drills in my book over and over until you master them. I have found that kids who can't skate are filled with frustration and anger and are likely to take needless penalties and get into fights. Better skating techniques will make for a better and safer game, as well as less injuries.

The skating or the physical part of a game is only half the battle. The other half is your mind and your attitude. You must always think positive in any situation in your game. "Positive begets positive" and "negative begets negative." If you listen to everything I tell you, then by the end of reading this book, I hope to have made a lasting impression, not only on your skating, but on your life as well.

Many coaches, parents, and hockey players ask me, "What exactly is power skating?" I tell them it is a system for using the edges of one's skate blades, basing all the movements on inside and outside edges, along with a procession of drills and exercises for balance and agility. All of these movements have to be done in a hockey stance: knees well bent under the player's shoulders with the chest up. Years ago, coaches would tell you to lean forward too much. That was wrong because there is too much weight put on your toes. The weight and push-off is on the ball of your foot. Also, if you lean too far forward, you are off balance and will fall and you cannot breathe correctly. I will explore proper stance more in depth later in my book.

Until then, know that power skating will not cure all the player's problems. Hockey is a highly skilled game because it is done on the ice in skates, unlike football, baseball, soccer, and lacrosse, which are done in sneakers or sports shoes. The more knowledgeable you are in skating techniques, the more skilled you will be in your game.

Enjoy my book and read it slowly.

See you in the NHL.

Barbara Williams

# CHAPTER 1
## ABOUT BARBARA WILLIAMS

Many people, as well as hockey players, are curious about how a girl from Brooklyn, New York could wind up being The First Female Skating Coach in the National Hockey League. Well, this is my story, and I hope it will answer many questions for the curious seeker.

I was born on Gerritsen Avenue, Brooklyn, New York on a hot summer day to Irish Catholic parents, Andrew and Christina. I have five siblings: three sisters (Maureen, Patricia, and Michelle) and two brothers (Andrew and Brian). I was the only child interested in sports. Since I was five years old, I wanted to be a famous skater, especially after seeing a documentary on TV about a young blonde Norwegian figure skating champion, Sonja Henie. I told my mother that one day I too would be on TV and I would be a famous skater and be in newspapers and magazines. Little did my mother know that even at five years old, I had made up my mind and that I was determined to fulfill my dream.

It wasn't until I moved from Brooklyn, New York to Manhasset, Long Island that I became serious about my sport. Coming from a wealthy family, my father could afford the best coaches to train me in figure skating: Howard Nicholson, and a wonderful British coach Vera Cross. I skated every day before school and after school. Skating was my life and my passion. But there was another side to me. I loved the feeling of going fast, so I joined The Flushing Meadow Bicycle Club, as well as a speed skating club. It was unusual to train in both sports, figure skating and speed skating, but I loved them both equally.

*Keep a kid busy and you'll keep him off the streets!*

My life growing up consisted of figure skating competitions, shows, and speed skating events, as well as schoolwork. Schoolwork was something that I disliked immensely, but I knew that I would go nowhere in life if I didn't graduate with honors. Also I knew my parents would ground me and take away my skates if I didn't have high marks. I had many tutors in school that helped me achieve my goals, and I did graduate with honors.

In my twenties, I turned professional and became Director of The Skating School at Racquet & Rink in Farmingdale, Long Island, New York.

*Barbara with her friend Gerrie Hotop*

It was in the late 1970s and this is where the New York Islanders practiced. I never followed hockey, and I knew nothing about the sport. The one thing that I did know was there were always a lot of fights on the ice and a lot of blood. The fans loved that because I would watch a game on TV and every time the players would drop their gloves the fans went wild. I also witnessed one of these fights first hand. I arrived at the rink early one morning, and I had some time so I went into the rink where the Islanders were practicing. A fight broke out and one of the players that was in the fight skated over to the barrier and he had a bloody mouth. I just stared at him. Before I knew it he spit his teeth out on the ice, right in front of me! I thought I was going to faint, and I felt sick to my stomach.

That scene stayed with me for a long time. Needless to say, I didn't watch the Islanders practice again for quite a while.

One day, I had to speak with one of my managers, and I was told he was in the rink. It was early in the morning, and I thought no one was in the rink. I went in and I couldn't believe my eyes. There on the ice was New York Islander Bobby Nystrom. He was working on inside and outside edges and some balance drills. I was shocked to see this. I never saw a hockey player working on skating drills. I waited to speak to him and told him how surprised I was to see this. He smiled and proceeded to tell me that he had trained with a woman named Laura Stamm, who was a figure skating coach. She worked on skating drills so that he would become a better skater. He told me it was "Power Skating"! I had never heard that term used before, and the fact that a pro-hockey player had trained with a woman was something that I could barely comprehend. Anyway, our conversation lasted all but five minutes and as Bobby was walking into the locker room, he turned around and said that maybe we could work together one day. I just stood there and nodded "yes," but I was actually saying to myself, "Barbara, are you crazy, you know nothing about power skating and zero about hockey." I knew that I had to somehow get in touch with this woman, Laura Stamm. I was only hoping and praying that she would help me. I finally got Laura's phone number and did get to speak with her. I was surprised that we had similar skating backgrounds. We were both figure skaters and ice dancers. Anyway, I explained to her that Bobby Nystrom had spoken so highly of her and now we were both skating in the same rink in Farmingdale, Long Island. I asked her if she could tell me about power skating and perhaps give me some drills to work on with Bobby. She explained that I had to take everything that I learned in figure skating on edges, balance, crossovers, etc., and just put a hockey stance to it. It seemed easy enough. I thanked her for helping me and giving me some good advice. When I think back now, it really must have hurt her that someone else was teaching her star pupil, so thank you Laura. Without your help and guidance, I would not have been able to teach Bobby and the rest of the New York Islanders.

The very next day, I purchased my first pair of hockey skates. I was used to wearing black skates because I speed skated my whole life in black skates. The skates felt a little weird to me; the boot and blade were so different from the figure skates and the speed skating blade. It took me most of the day to get used to them.

I was determined to work with Bobby Nystrom. After skating for a whole week on hockey skates, I was now ready to work with Bobby. The big day came, and I have to tell you I was so nervous. We started out slowly, and before I knew it, *my new career as a power skating coach was born.* All of my fellow figure skating coaches thought that I was crazy and that I was losing my mind, but after a few weeks, they accepted my new life and could see that Bobby was skating much better. Many of the other Islanders started skating with me, and before you knew it, I was training most of the team. A lot of the players would confide in me not only about their weaknesses but other problems as well. They told me because I was a female, it was easy for them to talk to me. I still believe to this day that having a coach of the opposite sex is much more beneficial. A lot of times, I would see the New York Islanders coach, Al Arbour, watching my teaching sessions and he would smile and give me a thumbs up. I felt good that he believed in me.

I will never forget the date. It was January 1977, and I drove to the rink early to work with the players. When I arrived, the parking lot was filled with news trucks, TV stations, and at least one hundred reporters. I sat in my car watching the scene and decided to drive around to the back of the rink. I was sure that they had made a big trade for a player. I proceeded into the rink and got my skates on. I could hear so much commotion in the lobby. Anyway, I made my way on to the ice and waited for the players to come out. All of a sudden, people were piling into the rink and coming on to the ice and making their way towards me with microphones, cameras, and note pads. I really did not know what was going on. When I saw Coach Al Arbour getting onto the ice, I felt much better. He skated over to me and said in a loud voice, that the New York Islanders had just named the First Female Skating Coach in the National Hockey League. Then he said, even louder, "Let me introduce you to her: Miss Barbara Williams." I thought I was going to pass out. For the first time in my life, my legs were numb and shaking. Reporters were all talking to me at once, people were taking my picture and interviewing me. *At that moment history was made, not only for me but also for all women.* My life would never be the same, right up until now, 2014. I was on such a whirlwind, doing TV shows, radio, guest appearances, newspaper articles, and national magazines. It was a time in my life that will stay with me forever.

*See it, believe it, and it will happen!*

**NEW YORK ISLANDERS NEWS RELEASE**

HAWLEY CHESTER
Publicity Director
1155 Conklin Street
Farmingdale, New York 11735
Business: (516) 694-5522

FOR RELEASE:  WEEKEND EDITIONS SAT-SUN  JANUARY 8-9, 1977

## NEW YORK ISLANDERS NAME FIRST FEMALE SKATING COACH IN THE NHL

UNIONDALE, L.I.---"We began experimenting with the idea of additional skating instruction for some of our players this summer, and the results have been outstanding," said New York Islanders General Manager William A. Torrey in making the announcement today that Ms. Barbara Williams has been named the official Power Skating instructor for the Islanders.

A native of Long Island, Ms. Williams started skating when she was five years old and received her initial training from the same man who had earlier coached the great Sonja Henie, Howard Nicholson. A former silver medalist (Dance) in figure skating, who has also received many awards for long distance speed skating from the Middle Atlantic Speed Skating Association, Ms. Williams turned professional at 22 years of age and worked under the directorship of James Tester of the Nassau County Skating School at the Christopher Morley Park in Manhasset, Long Island.

Five years later Ms. Williams was named Assistant Director of the Racquet & Rink Skating School in Farmingdale and shortly thereafter she was appointed head of the Power Skating School where she worked with the New York Islanders Youth Hockey Association. Even though Ms. Williams later moved on to become the Director of the Superior Ice Rink Skating School, it was during her stay at the Racquet & Rink that she became involved with the Islanders through their summer hockey school.

Islander forward Bobby Nystrom was instructing at the summer hockey school and requested a refresher course to improve his balance and speed. "I think the power skating instruction is wonderful for the young skaters coming up and for the professional players as well," said Nystrom, who is enjoying his best start ever with a club leading 18 goals after 36 games. "I have improved in balance and speed and can maneuver with less energy through the lessons."

In addition to working with the Islander players such as Bob Bourne, Dave Lewis and Bill MacMillan, Ms. Williams is also the head Power Skating instructor for the Suffolk County Youth Hockey Association, South Shore Youth Hockey and the Beaver Dam Youth Hockey Associations. "Skating is the name of the game in ice hockey. I believe that if a player learns to use his edges where bodyweight and balance should be, he will conserve energy, increase speed and be more effective to the team."

New York Islander coach Al Arbour, who has observed the improvement in his players that have been working with Ms. Williams since the season began is enthusiastic about the results, "It's my belief that if Barbara can work a few minutes a day with all of my players, it will be a tremendous boost for the second half of this season. I've seen steady improvement in (Bob) Nystrom and (Bob) Bourne ever since they started working with her at training camp."

BARBARA WILLIAMS
POWER SKATING INSTRUCTOR

## Nystrom Prize Pupil
# Islanders Hire Female As Club's Skating Coach

**BY HARRY KLAFF**

LONG ISLAND— When Bob Nystrom first walked into the Islanders' training camp back in 1972, he had one basic deficiency. He couldn't skate, at least up to NHL standards.

Consequently, the Islanders sent him out for lessons, but not the type that the average person takes when he laces up the blades for the first time.

Instead, Bob was programmed to take a course in power skating, something that is well recognized in hockey circles today, but was unheard when both Nystrom and the Islanders were in their rookie seasons. Nystrom worked hard at it, and by the next year was a competent performer. But a long way from what he and the Islanders thought he could be.

"When I was drafted, they told me my problem was skating, and I agreed with them," said Nystrom. "The original power skating lessons helped immensely. I used to fall down a lot, even with no one near me."

This summer, Nystrom and other Islanders took a "refresher course" at the club's practice facility at Racquet and Rink in Farmingdale, N.Y. under pro Ms. Barbara Williams.

That's right, professional hockey players taking skating lessons from a woman. And you'd better believe that some of them were a little leary about that sort of arrangement, especially at the beginning. But it didn't take long before the players began to realize the success of the program, and then they didn't care who might have been watching.

Early in January Ms. Williams was officially appointed by general manager Bill Torrey as the official power skating coach of the Islanders. In a way, this is an extension of the arrangement that has existed all along, but now participation on the part of the Islanders might not be so voluntary. She's the coach and the boys have to listen.

"We began experimenting with the idea of additional skating instruction for some of our players this summer, and the results have been outstanding," said Torrey. "If Barbara can work with all of the players for only a few minutes a day, I think it will be a tremendous boost for the second half of the season."

Ms. Williams is a Long Island native, and received her early training from Howard Nicholson, the man who once coached Sonja Henie. She excelled in all phases of amateur competition, from speed skating to figure skating, and eventually turned to the teaching end. Five years ago she became the assistant director of Racquet and Rink's skating school.

Although Bob Bourne, Dave Lewis, Billy MacMillan, and Billy Harris have profitted from Barbara's tutelage, it is Nystrom who has been the prize pupil. A 20-goal scorer in each of the past three seasons, Nystrom has hit his stride this year, and is a threat for the 40-goal plateau.

"There's no question that the skating lessons have been a big help," continued Nystrom. "Let's face it, skating is the one part of the game that we really don't have much of a chance to practice on a regular basis. With power skating you concentrate on such things as using your edges more and keeping your balance. It's something that you work at over and over again."

Bobby was in an exceptionally happy mood on Jan. 10 as his three goals helped sink the Philadelphia Flyers, 8-3 at the Nassau Coliseum before a national TV audience. His first two goals of the evening came on a screen shot from the slot and a tip-in, but it was the third that made Barbara Williams break into a wide grin.

He took a pass from Bourne near the Flyer line, carried in with a defenseman on his back, deked, deked, and deked again until Bernie Parent was flat on the ice then slip the Isles an insurmountable 6-2 lead, which set the stage for a happy celebration for the fans that lasted throughout the final 20 minutes.

Power skating may not be the missing link to the Stanley Cup, but it has helped contribute a winning attitude. And that's a giant step in the right direction.

**ISLAND SOUNDS:** Denis Potvin played his best game of the year against Philly, collecting a goal and two assists in addition to playing a strong defensive game...Bryan Trottier's been playing with torn ligaments in his elbow, but hasn't affected his game any...Isles broke out with three power play goals against Philly...Lorne Henning's fourth shorthanded goal of the season gave Isles a victory over Atlanta prior to the Philadelphia battle...Islander Booster Club dinner-dance scheduled for Feb. 10.

**BOB NYSTROM... Passes "Refresher Course"**

# SPORTS PEOPLE
Photos by Anthony Casale

## Power Behind Islanders

"I don't teach hockey, I teach skating." When 5-foot-2, 117-pound Barbara Williams teaches, 6-foot, 200-pound jocks listen. Barbara is the Islanders' new power skating coach — the first woman coach in the NHL. A no-nonsense instructor, Barbara works the tails off the Isles, mostly in individual sessions. If they resent it, they don't dare show it. They know she's tough—and a lot prettier, too.

Following a team practice at the Racquet & Rink Arena on the Island, coach Al Arbour goes over skating assignments with Barbara.

An intense worker who takes her new assignment very seriously, Barbara sits on a desk in her office to study roster and progress charts before hitting the ice.

## By JACK SAUNDERS  United Press International

*Credits the Islanders skating instructor Barbara Williams with the improvement in his balance and skating this season.*

*Barbara training NY Islanders Bobby Bourne, Dave Lewis, & Bobby Nystrom*

*Barbara training NY Islanders Bobby Bourne & Dave Lewis*

The months that followed flew by. I was very comfortable in training the players, and we got to be good friends. There were a few memorable incidents that took place. Like the time one player needed tape and he asked me to get it for him in the locker room. I ran into the locker room and right into another player getting out of the shower. You could hear me scream from Long Island to Canada. Of course, the players were hysterically laughing. Another funny story was when I was doing a referee clinic. A brochure was sent out to meet B. Williams in the locker room. I walked into the locker room, and there in front of me was an older gentleman in his underwear. He screamed at me asking me what I was doing there. I replied "What are you doing here?" He said he was meeting B. Williams to do the ref. clinic. I replied in a loud voice, "I am B. Williams!" He had a look of shock on his face and politely said, "I thought B. Williams was a guy." At that point, about 10 to 15 refs began walking into the locker room fully dressed, staring at us. They said, "What the heck was going on in here?!?" We all started laughing at once.

*Barbara Training NY Islander John Tonnelli*

*Bobby Nystrom Scoring the 1980 Stanely Cup Winning Goal*

But I guess the most profound memory that I have was Bobby Nystrom scoring the winning goal in the 1980 Stanley Cup playoffs. That will stay with me forever, and just to know that I trained him made me feel so proud.

My years with the New York Islanders were truly amazing and so rewarding. I published my first book (MacMillan Publishing) *More Power to Your Skating.*

I went on a national book tour while I was promoting my book. I trained hundreds of figure skating coaches to become power skating coaches for youth hockey.

*Suzie Belliveau, Felita Yost, Barbara, Kim Lynch, & Liz Eldridge*

*Barbara training Movie Star Robbie Benson*

I trained movie star, Robbie Benson, for his starring role in *Ice Castles* and received full screen credits.

*NHL New Jersey Devils Skating Coach Barbara Williams*

After the New York Islanders, I went on to becoming the Official Skating Coach to the NHL New Jersey Devils. I also coached four NHL farm teams and trained hundreds of NHL pros privately.

It is now 2014, and my career is still going strong. I have many players in the NHL and, more importantly, Division I and Division III colleges on full scholarships. I also have my own summer hockey school on Long Island, which has been a success for the past 25 years.

*2013 Summer Hockey School*
*Brendan Riley, Jack Adams, Barbara, Charles Sikorski, and Merritt Riley*

*Barbara's 2013 Hockey School*

*This is Barbara's favorite picture from when she was with the NY Islanders with Chris Goodrich and David Ramirez.*

*Suffolk Sports Hall of Fame 2011 Inductee*

I was inducted in 2011 into The Sports Hall of Fame in Suffolk County, Long Island. I currently skate six hours a day and preach positive thinking to all my students, as well as life lessons on respect, morals, compassion, kindness, fortitude, and most importantly to have faith in your life. Faith will make you strong and you will be able to handle anything. For me personally, I thank Jesus Christ my Lord and Savior every day for my children, family, health, and career.

God bless each and every one of you.

Barbara Williams

# CHAPTER 2
## GETTING IN SHAPE

*Jon DiFlorio*

**Institute 3E** is an elite off-ice training center in Huntington, NY and the Twin Rinks at Eisenhower Park in East Meadow, NY. The highly-trained staff specializes in helping players of all levels achieve success on and off the ice. Using a unique approach, **Institute 3E** integrates hockey-specific strength and conditioning, mental edge coaching, and nutrition and lifestyle guidance to create a complete program designed specifically to meet the needs of each athlete.

Traditional strength training often fails to include key elements that are essential for continued athletic development. New discoveries in sports science are shedding light on ways to achieve peak performance. **Institute 3E** is on the cutting edge of these developing approaches and has successfully implemented programs for hockey athletes of all ages and skill levels including Tier 1 Amateur, Junior, NCAA, and NHL players.

<u>**No one**</u> **is more committed to athletic success than Institute 3E.**

**Jon DiFlorio** is the founder of Institute 3E and has worked with a wide variety of athletes including athletes in the NFL, MLB, MLL, and NHL.

The following are a few notable NHL clients that Jon has worked with:

- Eric Nystrom, *Nashville Predators*
- Chris Higgins, *Vancouver Canucks*
- Mike Komisarek, *Carolina Hurricanes (NHL All-star 08'/09')*
- Bill Guerin, *Pittsburgh Penguins (Stanley Cup Winner 08'/09')*
- Matt Gilroy, *Florida Panthers*
- Rick DiPietro, *New York Islanders (NHL All-star 07'/08')*

In 2005 Jon was chosen to assist the Toronto Maple Leafs "Prospect Camp" to share his expertise in assessment, program design, and exercise instruction. Additionally, he has lectured for several organizations including Designs For Health "Clinical Rounds" (Sports Nutrition), ATINER International Conference on Sports (Standard Functional Assessment), Hofstra University (Assessment and Program Design/Sports Nutrition), and the American College of Sports Medicine (Standard Functional Assessment).

**Credentials:**
Certified Strength & Conditioning Specialist (CSCS); Weightlifting Club Coach (USAW); Poliquin Certified (PICP) Level 4; Corrective Holistic Exercise Kinesiologist (CHEK) level III; CHEK Holistic Lifestyle Coach (HLC); Biosignature & Lab Analysis Practitioner; Poliquin Certified in Instant Muscle Strengthening Techniques (PIMST).

*You control your own destiny!*

# OFF-ICE TRAINING

The best way to make sure on-ice performance will continually improve from Mite to Junior level is by introducing a well-rounded fitness plan at a young age (8-10). The fitness program should focus on specific exercises known as *GENERAL COORDINATION* and *FUNDAMENTAL MOVEMENT SKILLS*. These exercises will be referred to below as "**BUILDING BLOCK EXERCISES**" because they will serve as the foundation for hockey development.

When designing this type of exercise program, one must work to master the easier, *basic exercises* before moving on to more difficult, *complex exercises*. Here are a few examples:

**Building Block Exercises**

*Basic Exercises:*
- *Crawling (all varieties)*
- *Walking*
- *Running (all directions)*
- *Skipping (forward)*
- *Hopping (all directions)*
- *Jumping (focus on the take off and landing)*
- *Somersault*
- *Climbing (steps/monkey bars/rope with knots)*
- *Chin-up/pull-up (holds)*
- *Single leg balance (holds)*
- *Headstands (tripod)*
- *Cartwheels*
- *Push-ups (negatives and holds)*
- *Overhead squats (dowel)*
- *Lunging*
- *Throwing, kicking, hitting with a stick or racquet*

*Complex Exercises:*

- *Skipping (for height or sideways/backward/diagonal)*
- *Jump rope*
- *Dodging*
- *Jumps to a box*
- *Broad jump*
- *Jump down from a box*
- *Handstands*
- *Cartwheels (multiple/weak side)*
- *Rope climbing*
- *Chin-up/Pull-up for repetitions*
- *Somersault to standing*
- *Push-ups*
- *Throwing, kicking or hitting off the run*
- *Olympic lifting progressions (dowel)*
- *Lunging (multiple directions)*
- *Single leg balance with reaching or eyes closed*
- *Long jump*

Incomplete development of general coordination skills, weak muscles, poor flexibility, and bad posture are the most common challenges a hockey player must overcome to become a great skater. Often times, an athlete cannot do what a coach is telling him/her to do because of one or more of these limitations.

For example, a coach may tell the player, "Bend your knees and get lower," but if the athlete is too tight, he may not physically be able to get lower, even if he tries his hardest!

The most common skating flaws are: rounded shoulders, leaning too far forward, knees too straight, and thrust too wide. Find your skating flaw on the chart and look for the exercises and stretches that are checked off within that column. Create an exercise program that combines a variety of general coordination exercises with exercises that address your specific skating flaw(s).

# SKATING FLAW

## EXERCISES

| | Rounded Shoulders | Leaning Too Far Forward | Knees too Straight | Thrust too Wide | Improve Change of Direction | Improve Explosive Power |
|---|---|---|---|---|---|---|
| Prone Cobra | √ | √ | | | | |
| Side Step Up | | √ | √ | √ | √ | |
| Front Squat | √ | √ | √ | | | √ |
| Dead lift | √ | √ | √ | | | √ |
| Walking lunge with a twist | | √ | √ | √ | | √ |
| Front Step Up | | √ | √ | √ | √ | |
| Hexagon Deadlift | √ | √ | √ | | | |
| Overhead Squat | √ | √ | √ | | | |
| Jump to Box | | | | | | √ |
| Side Sled Drag | | | | √ | √ | |
| One Arm Row | √ | √ | | | | |
| Face Pulls | √ | √ | | | | |
| Chin Up | | | | | | √ |
| Rope Climbing | | | | | | √ |
| Split Squat | √ | √ | √ | | | |
| Broad Jump | | | | | | √ |
| Back Extension with Eccentric Overload | √ | √ | | | | |
| Reverse Back Extension | √ | √ | | | | |

# STRENGTH EXERCISES

### Prone Cobra (5-6 repetitions): *Beginner*
***Will help address the following skating flaws: Rounded shoulders, leaning too far forward.**

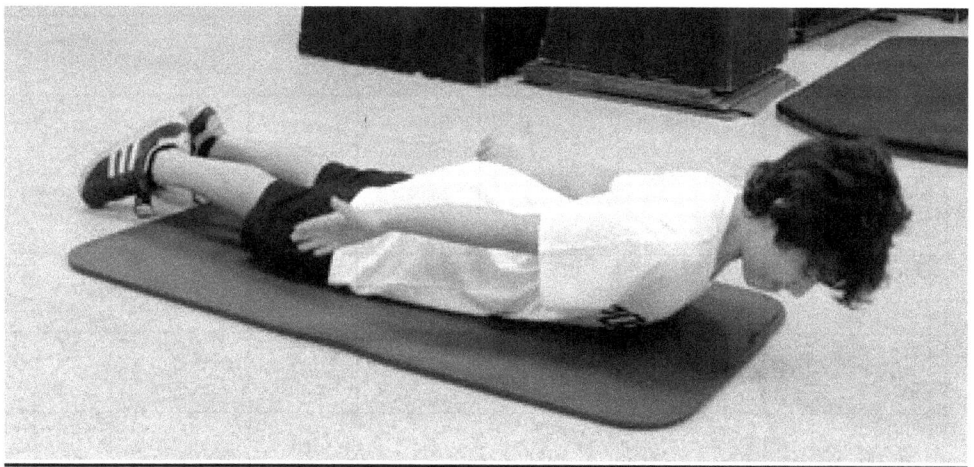

Step 1: Lay face down on your stomach with your arms rested at your sides.

Step 2: Raise your upper body and arms toward the ceiling, while keeping your waist on the ground. Keep your neck and head in line with your back.

Step 3: At the same time, rotate your arms out so that your palms face out and your thumbs point up.

Step 4: Hold your body and arms up for thirty seconds.

Step 5: Bring your body and arms down and rest for fifteen seconds.

## Side step up (10-15 repetitions): *Beginner/Intermediate*

**\*Will help address the following skating flaws: Leaning too far forward, knees too straight, thrust too wide, improve change of direction.**

Step 1: Stand up straight with one leg on an elevated platform. Toes slightly pointed outward.

Step 2: The opposite leg should be off the platform, knees straight with toes pointing upward.

Step 3: Lower yourself so the heel of the stiff leg taps the floor.

Step 4: Upon tap, return to the start position only using the leg on the platform.

\*Reminder→Only the leg on the platform should be doing work. Do not push off the floor with the opposite leg.

*Do not say the words "I can't." Say "I can!"*

# Front Squat *Intermediate/Advanced*

**\*Will help address the following skating flaws: Rounded shoulders, leaning too far forward, knees too straight, improve explosive power.**

Step 1: Approach the rack and place your hands under the bar, palms up, and elbows pointing forward. With only your fingertips holding the bar in place, have the bar resting completely on your shoulders.

Step 2: Once the bar is lifted, set up for the descent by placing your feet at shoulder width apart, and very slightly rotated outward. Your heels must remain planted on the floor throughout the entire exercise.

Step 3: Initiate the descent by first bending your knees followed by your hips. Lower deep into the squat until your calves and hamstrings meet, and your body cannot go any lower. Make sure your hips are lower than your knees before you come back up.

Step 4: Push the weight aggressively back up to the starting position.

\*Reminder→ Keep your heels flat on the floor for the duration of the movement.
Maintain a tall posture, and rigid spine, with your chest out to support the weight of the bar. The barbell has to rest comfortably on your shoulders and not your hands.

\*\***WARNING**→ If you can't lower your backside past your knees, you should not attempt the front squat with additional weight!

## Deadlift: *Intermediate/Advanced*

**\*Will help address the following skating flaws: Rounded shoulders, leaning too far forward, knees too straight, improve explosive power.**

Step 1: Stand at the barbell, with feet about hip width.

Step 2: Squat down to grip the barbell, while slightly leaning forward. Make sure your shoulders are over the bar and your knees are behind.

Step 3: Make sure your back is flat and in line with your neck when grabbing the bar.

Step 4: Grip the bar outside of your knees, with your hands on top of the bar.

Step 5: With straight arms, and a straight back, lift the barbell by straightening your legs.

Step 6: Once the barbell passes the mid-thigh, straighten your entire body, as you thrust your hips forward and roll your shoulders back.

Step 7: Return the bar to the floor using the same steps in reverse order. Repeat from step 2.

## Walking lunge with twist: *Intermediate*

*Will help address the following skating flaws: Knees too straight, leaning too far forward, thrust (too wide).

Step 1: Begin balancing on your left leg with your right leg behind you and the ball over your head.

Step 2: While keeping your upper body upright, step forward with your right leg while holding the ball to the right, ending with your left knee brushing the ground and your torso twisted to the right. Do not rest on your left knee.

Step 3: Step forward with your left leg while keeping your left knee well bent. Twist your upper body to the left holding the ball.

Step 4: Repeat the sequence in a series of lunges.

---

*Want a career in the NHL? Study, study, study!
Keep your marks up in school!*

**Front Step-Up:** *Beginner/Intermediate*

*Will help address the following skating flaws: Knees too straight, thrust too wide, improve change of direction.

Find a platform high enough to form a 90 degree angle between your upper and lower leg when you place your foot on top. Your hands should be at your sides, with palms facing your legs. Dumbbells may be used.

Step 1: Face the platform and place your front foot flat on it. Your back leg should be straight, with the foot flat on the floor, a few inches from the platform. Point your front foot comfortably on the platform and keep your shoulders back and head up, looking forward.

Step 2: Stand up by straightening your front leg to support your weight. Once you are on top of the platform and not on the ground, your back leg should be straightened as well, and pointed a few inches away from your base.

Step 3: Slowly return yourself to starting position. In order to maintain balance, avoid crossing legs.

*Positive thinking makes you feel stronger and confident!*

## Hexagon Deadlift *Intermediate*

**\*Will help address the following skating flaws: Rounded shoulders, leaning too far forward, knees too straight.**

Step 1: Bend down to the hexagon barbell with feet hip width apart and make sure your lower back is level with your knees.

Step 2: Make sure your back is completely straight when grabbing the bar (neck has to be in line with back).

Step 3: Grip the bar with an overhand grip.

Step 4: Pull the bar up by straightening your legs first with long arms and then by your whole body once the weight passes the mid-thigh point.

\*Reminder→ Be aware while squatting down: have your knees point forward so that your using leg power instead of your back being used.

*Have a dream and believe!*

## Overhead Squat *Beginner*

**\*Will help address the following skating flaws: Rounded shoulders, knees too straight, leaning too far forward.**

 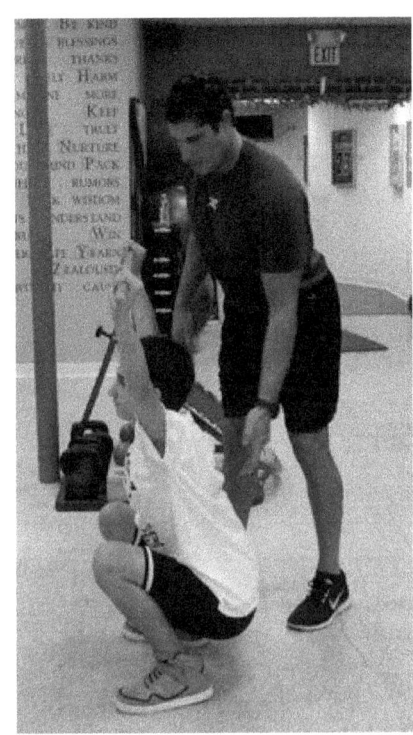

Step 1: Grip barbell 4-6 inches wider than shoulder width.

Step 2: Raise the barbell over your head, with your arms straight and elbows locked.

Step 3: Make sure your back is completely straight when grabbing the bar (neck has to be in line with spine).

Step 4: Sit back so that your rear ends comes out, and make sure your knees are pointed outward.

Step 5: While squatting down, make sure your rear end passes below knee level.

Step 6: Explosively rise up with the bar above your head by straightening your legs.

\*Reminder→ Make sure your knees are pointed outward while squatting down. The bar has to be in line with the mid point of your foot.

\*\***WARNING**→ If you can't bring your backside below knee level, you should not attempt the overhand squat.

## Jump to Box *Intermediate/Advanced*
**\*Will help improve explosive power.**

Step 1: Stand in front of a desired platform. The height will vary with experience. Start with your feet at shoulder width apart, at a comfortable distance from the platform.

Step 2: With your arms in an overhead position, lower yourself as if you were beginning a squat. Swing your arms down and back to generate momentum, then jump up by pushing through the floor, extending your legs and pushing your arms upward, moving forward to the platform.

Step 3: Soften the landing on the platform by bending your knees and bringing your hands back to your center. You should land in a position very similar to how you began the jump: in a shallow squat position.

Step 4: Lightly hop off of the platform into the ready position to repeat the exercise.

\*Reminder→ This should be a full body effort, done with the same intensity and resting patterns as any other exercise.

\*\***WARNING**→ Make sure you are comfortable and performing the exercise correctly before adding any weight.

## Side Sled Drag: *Beginner/Intermediate*

**\*Will help address the following skating flaws: Thrust too wide and improve ability to change direction.**

Step 1: Set up the sled with a comfortable weight. Start with it on one side of you.

Step 2: Place the belt around your waist and attach it about 5 feet away from the sled.

Step 3: At a steady and strong pace, step away from the sled, starting with the foot on the sled side, so that your sled-side leg crosses over the opposite leg.

Step 4: Follow with the opposite leg.

Step 5: Continue until a specific distance/time is reached.

Step 6: Switch sides and repeat.

\*Reminder→ These motions must be done powerfully and you must stay low for the most effective results. Try to focus on using one leg at a time.

*Look in the mirror and see your potential.
Nothing can hold you back, only yourself.*

## One arm Row: *Intermediate*

*Will help address the following skating flaws: Rounded shoulders, leaning too far forward.

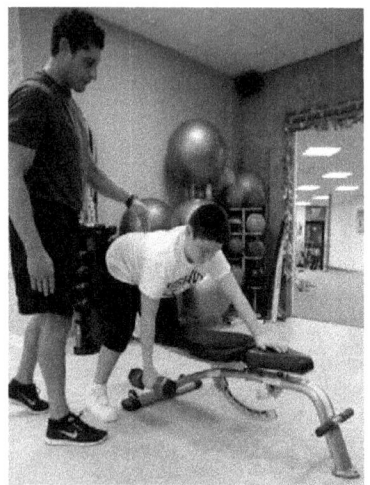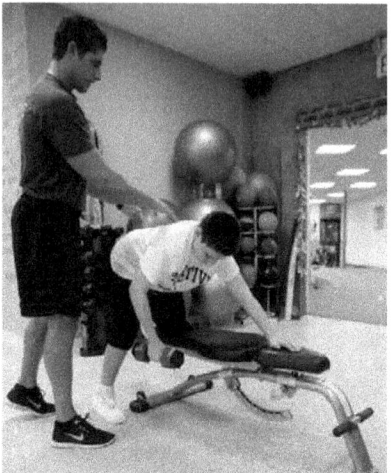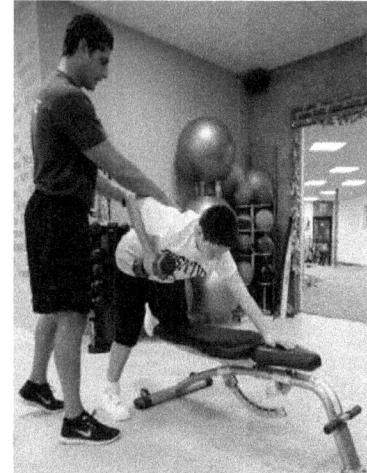

Step 1: Place one knee and arm of the same side of your body on the bench to brace yourself.

Step 2: Keep your hips, chest, and shoulder inline with each other and parallel to the floor. Chin tucked, neck flat, lengthen your spine as much as possible.

Step 3: Beginning with a straight arm, lift your elbow, and the weight, as high as possible (at least bringing your elbow level with your back). And then lower back down to the straight-arm position.

*Reminder→ Only your arms should be moving, keep your stomach tight, and your back and neck straight. You should be bent at the hips, not the lower back.

*Every dream starts with an idea and a thought.*

## Face Pulls: *Beginner/Intermediate*

***Will help address the following skating flaws: Rounded shoulders, leaning too far forward.**

Step 1: Stand facing a cable pulley system with a split stance.

Step 2: With knees slightly bent, back and neck straight, and a tight stomach, grasp a rope attachment or bar attachment on the cable machine with an overhand grip at face level. Elbows should be slightly lower or even with your shoulders.

Step 3: Pull the cable directly towards your face, bending your arms at the elbows and forming a right angle with the cable and your upper arms. At this point, the cable should be directly in line with your eyes and nose.

Step 4: Slowly return your arms to starting position while keeping your elbows at an even level with your shoulders.

---

*One "positive thought" can set a whole new future in motion.*

## Chin-Ups: *Beginner/Intermediate/Advanced*
**\*Will help improve explosive power.**

Chin-ups help hockey players to withstand high levels of force acting against them. It is also one of the best exercises to improve slap shot power.

Step 1: Start by grabbing the bar with a shoulder width grip or slightly narrower. Palms should be facing your body.

Step 2: Arms must be completely straight in a hanging position to begin the movement.

Step 3: Pull yourself up explosively by flexing your arms and shoulders, lifting yourself to the point where your chin passes the bar. When you are at the highest position, your chin should be above the bar.

Step 4: Slowly lower yourself back to the starting position until your arms are completely straight, breathing out as you descend.

## Rope Climbing: *Intermediate*
### *Will help improve explosive power.
Rope climbing is one of the best upper body exercises.

Step 1: Grab the rope with both hands even with your head.

Step 2: Wrap your feet around the rope, crossing them once in place, place one foot on top of the other so your feet pinch the rope in place. The rope should be between the top of one foot, and the middle of the bottom of the other.

Step 3: Reach up with one hand first, and then reach up with the other.

Step 4: You should lean back and let the rope slide through your feet. Pull your knees up towards your stomach while supporting your weight with your arms. Once your knees are as high as you can bring them:

Step 5: Pinch the rope again between your feet and straighten out your legs while pulling up with your arms at the same time.

Step 6: Travel up the rope as high as you can.

Step 7: Return to the ground by keeping your legs straight and your feet clasped around the rope. Lower yourself hand-over-hand until you are back down on the ground.

**WARNING→ Always avoid sliding down the rope to avoid rope burn on your hands or legs. Save enough energy to return to the ground.

## Split Squat: *Beginner*

**\*Will help address the following skating flaws: Leaning too far forward, rounded shoulders, knees too straight.**

Step 1: Start by putting one foot forward.

Step 2: Your feet should be hip width apart, and in a split position, far enough to comfortably carry out the exercise.

Step 3: This may be done with body weight or a dumbbell in each hand, using weight that will allow maximum range of motion.

Step 4: Hold your hands at your side, and in the case of using dumbbells, with your palms facing you.

Step 5: Keep your back and neck straight, your chest up, shoulders back, and head looking straight ahead.

Step 6: Slowly lower yourself far enough to bring your front knee past your front foot. You should be as low as you can be with your back knee gently touching the ground. Your entire front foot should be touching the surface, while your back foot's heel should be raised off the ground at your lowest point. Your back knee should be slightly bent.

Step 7: Straighten both legs and return to starting position.

*Reminder → You should complete all of the reps with one leg forward before reversing leg position.

## Broad Jumps: *Beginner/Intermediate/Advanced*

**\*Will help improve explosive power.**

Step 1: Start with your feet shoulder width apart.

Step 2: In one powerful motion:

    A) Slightly bend your knees and swing your arms back, then:

    B) Swing your arms forward and jump forward as far as you can.

\*Reminder→ Try to land comfortably and controlled to avoid injury.

## Back Extension-with Eccentric Overload: *Beginner*

**\*Will help address the following skating flaws: Rounded shoulders, leaning too far forward, and will improve thrust.**

Step 1: Start stomach down on the glute-ham device with your hips resting on the pad comfortably, positioned so that you will have a free range of motion bending forward at the hips. Keep both legs between the back bars with your feet flat against the platform so that you are supported throughout the exercise.

Step 2: If you can, grasp a comfortable amount of weight in your hands and hold it close to your chest.

Step 3: Bend forward slowly at the hips. Maintain a straight back and neck, and keep your head in line with the rest of your spine. Continue forward as far as you can comfortably go, while being able to return.

Step 4: Reverse the motion in a controlled movement using your lower back muscles until your upper body is in line with your legs. Then repeat.

\*Reminder→ Start with, and become comfortable with, body weight before adding additional weight to the exercise.

*Live your dreams!*

## Reverse Back Extension: *Beginner*

**\*Will help address the following skating flaws: Knees too straight, leaning too far forward, rounded shoulders, and will improve thrust.**

 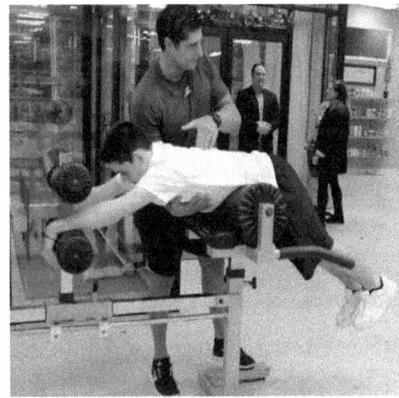 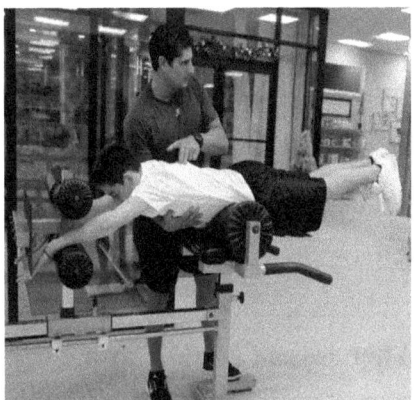

Step 1: Start turned around on the glute-ham device so that your waist is still supported on the flat pad, but this time your arms will be facing the leg support bars, with your hands grasping them.
Step 2: Start with your legs straight out, in line with the rest of your body. Keep your head down, in line with your neck and spine.
Step 3: While having your legs together and straight, with your feet pointing behind you, slowly lower your legs to the ground, bending at the hips.
Step 4: Lower your legs until they are about to reach the ground, then pause before your feet touch the ground. Do not touch the ground.
Step 5: Return your legs to the starting position, in line with your upper body, at a slow and controlled pace. Then repeat.

Reminder→ Take your time.

# Bio- Jessica Raddock

After Jessica's career as a competitive figure skater for 11 years, she studied exercise science at Hofstra University in the pursuit of contributing to the sport from a slightly different angle. She was inspired to use corrective exercise off-ice to improve skating performance. Institute 3E has provided her the opportunity to work with skaters using a relatively innovative approach to the sport. Since 2010, she has been actively studying under Dr. Guy Voyer D.O., learning, practicing, and implementing techniques such as Myofascial Stretching, ELDOA, and other forms of corrective exercise taught in the Soma Training program. After the athlete has been carefully assessed, Jessica creates a detailed program with various exercise techniques based on the needs of the individual skater. Decreasing potential injury risk, increasing mobility in certain areas and improving postural deviations are two key components she focuses on. Improvements associated with corrective work off the ice often influences how a skater executes elements on-ice and may even correct common skating flaws.

Credentials: B.S. Exercise Science, Weightlifting Club Coach (USAW), BioSignature Practitioner, CrossFit Level I Coach.

# Stretching

The type of stretching in these examples is called myofascial stretching (MFS). Before stretching, be sure to warm-up properly. It is important to *wake-up* the joints and to start stretching with your heart rate elevated. The goal of MFS is to improve movement based on the athletes' goals and limitations. Therefore, they must work within a certain range of difficulty. It is important not to push too hard past this point or into a range where a stretch may become injurious, overstretching a muscle. Hold each stretch for about 20 seconds in a steady position without any bouncing.

<u>**Butterflies:**</u>
**Will help address the following flaws:** *Rounded shoulders, Leaning too far forward*
    **Position**:
        **Step 1:** Lying on your stomach with one side of face pressed onto mat.
        **Step 2:** Palms facing down with your arms forming a V-shape.
        **Step 3:** Maintain a flat back with straight legs.

    **Exercise**:
        **Step 1:** Raising your arms up, straight and high.
        **Step 2:** Go slowly for 10 repetitions.
        **Step 3:** Face the opposite direction and repeat.
***Increase the number of sets each week until you can do 5 sets, 15-20 times each side.

## Muscles of Chest Stretch (Pectoralis Major)

**Will help address the following flaws:** *Rounded shoulders.*

### Position:

**Step 1:** Lie on your stomach with one side of your face pressing on the mat.

**Step 2**: Place one arm at an angle and extend it straight.

**Step 3:** Bend your other arm and keep it the same level as your neck.

\*\*\* Be sure to have your cheek turned to the side of the bent arm.

### Exercise:

**Step 1:** Take the arm that is straight and roll your shoulder forward into the mat.

**Step 2:** Flex your wrist and extend your fingers up and towards the ceiling.

**Step 3:** Hold stretch for 20-30 seconds and then switch to the other side.

\*\*\*It is normal to feel a tingling or shooting feeling through your fingers. This will go away with practice.

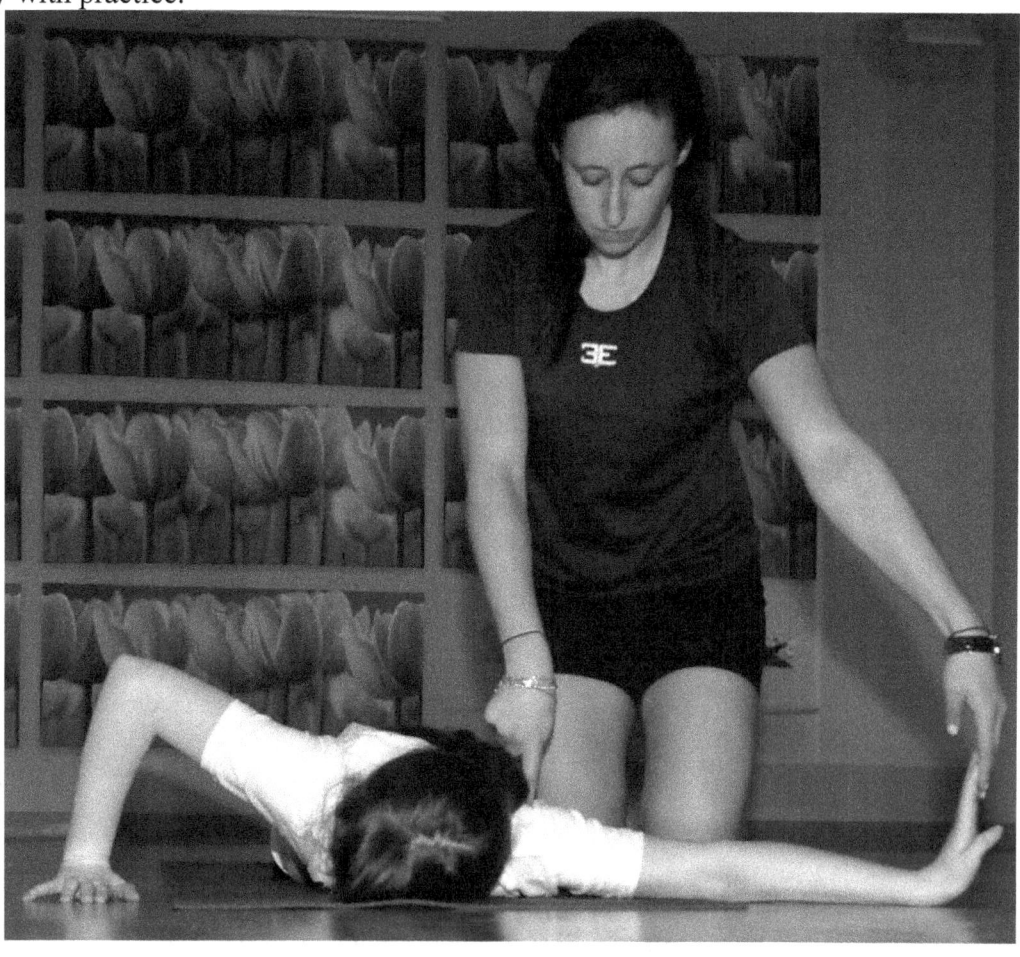

## Hip Rotator Stretch (90/90 Stretch)

**Will help address the following flaws:** *Thrust too wide.*

**Position:**

**Step 1:** Sit down on mat.

**Step 2:** Place one leg at 90 degrees in front and the other at 90 degrees behind.

**Step 3:** Torso should be in the center of both legs.

**Exercise:**

**Step 1:** Push the back hip down into mat and the front knee down at same time.

**Step 2:** Extend the arm of the back leg arm in front.

***Progression: Extend both arms in line with the torso.

# Hip Flexor Stretch

**Will help address the following flaws:** *Leaning too far forward*

**Position:** "Kneeling knight position" *(Similar to a skating lunge.)*

**Step 1:** Front knee bent with your knee over your toes.

**Step 2:** Spread feet far apart.

**Step 3:** Tuck your hips under.

**Step 4:** Keep your back flat.

**Step 5:** Your back foot should be flat on mat with your heel facing up.

**Exercise:**

**Step 1:** Come forward with chest.

**Step 2:** Extend both arms forward with palms out and fingers down.

## Glute Stretch:

**Will help address the following flaws:** *Thrust too wide.*

### Position:

**Step 1:** Lie on your back.

**Step 2:** Cross one leg over the other.

**Step 3:** Reach behind one leg, grabbing behind the bottom thigh.

### Exercise:

**Step 1:** Push the bent crossed leg away from torso towards the foot of the leg you are holding.

**Step 2:** Hold stretch 20 seconds and switch sides.

**Step 3:** Repeat 3 times.

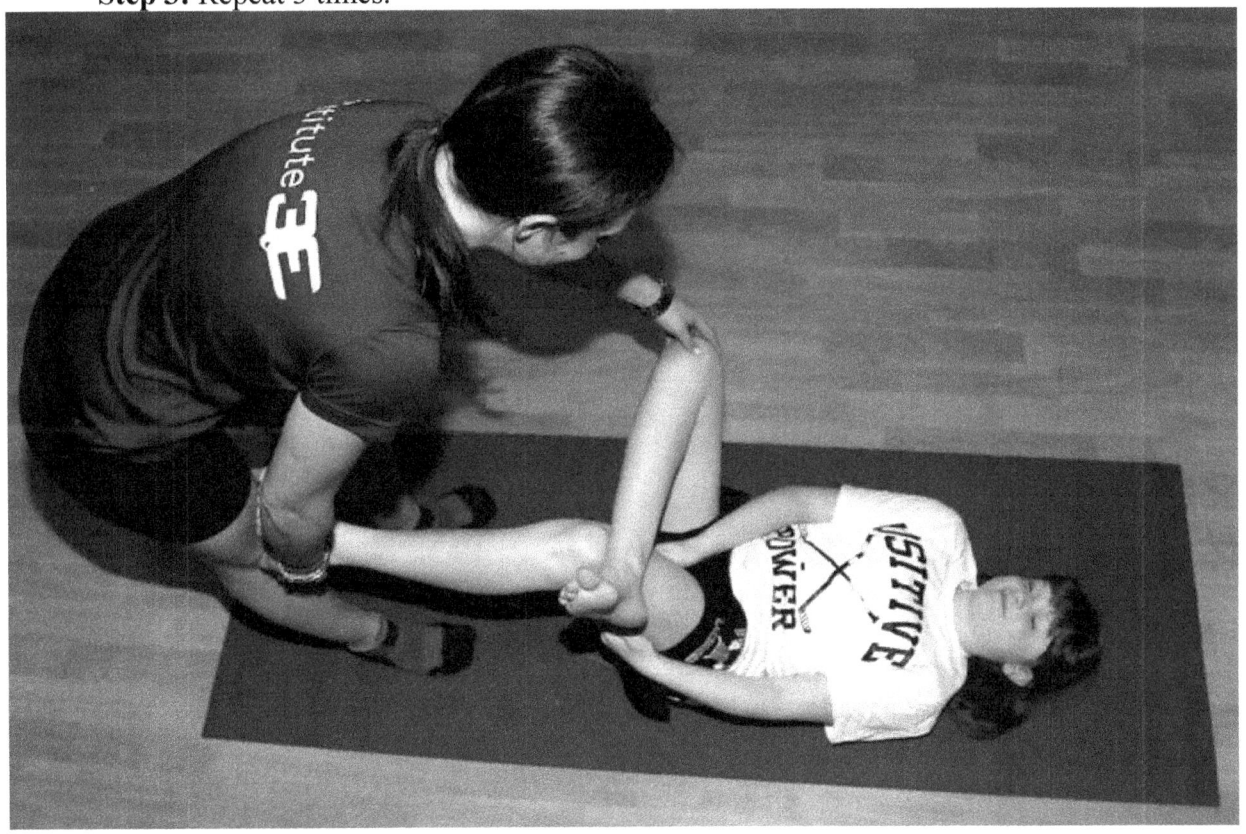

## Side of Hip Stretch

**Position:** Lying on your side, take the top leg and cross it in front of you. Place your foot on the floor (as flat as possible). Place the bottom leg on 3-4 yoga blocks at the level of your shin.

**Exercise:** Push heel of bottom leg into yoga blocks with toes facing up towards the ceiling.

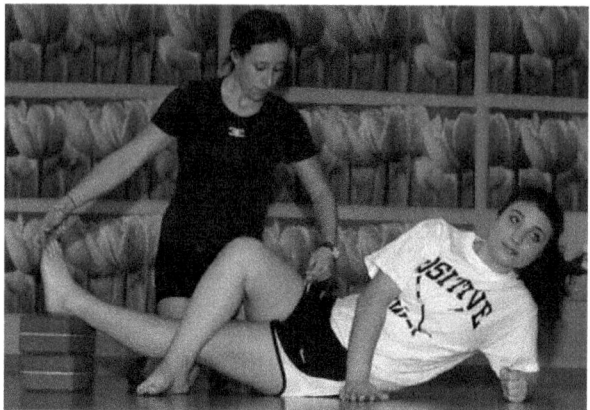

## Calf Stretch

**Position:** Push your hands into the wall with one leg in front of the other. Bend your front knee and keep the back leg straight. Foot of back leg should be turned towards the wall.

**Exercise:** Push hands into wall, place heel of back leg into floor while keeping the knee of back leg straight. Knee of front leg is bent using a wide stance. Hold for 10-30 seconds each side and repeat 3 times.

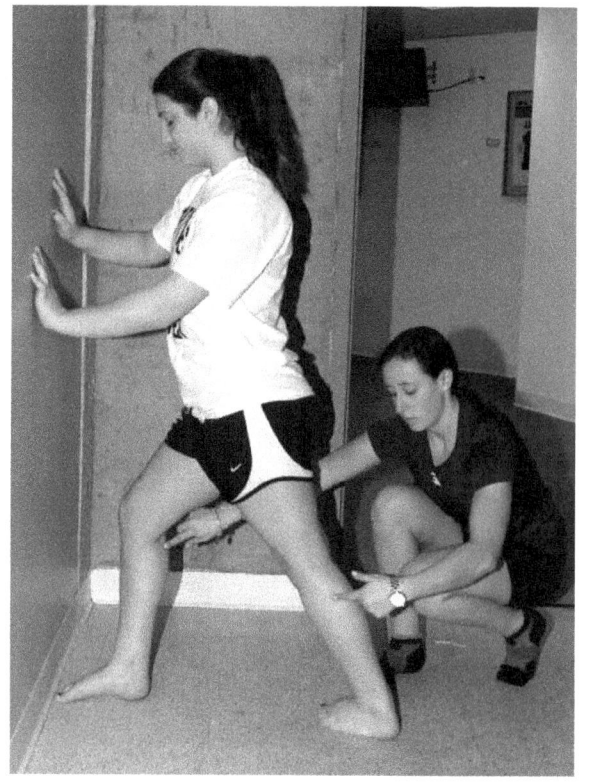

## Back of Leg Stretch (Hamstrings)

**Position:**

**Step 1:** Place 3 yoga blocks 3-5 inches in front of you.

**Step 2:** Feet are turned in (pigeon toed).

**Step 3:** Keep knees straight.

**Step 4:** Tuck chin in.

**Exercise:**

**Step 1:** Reach towards the floor with a curved back.

**Step 2:** Place your weight onto the block.

**Step 3:** Hold for 15-20 seconds.

**Step 4:** Bend your knees before you stand up.

**Step 5:** Repeat 3 times.

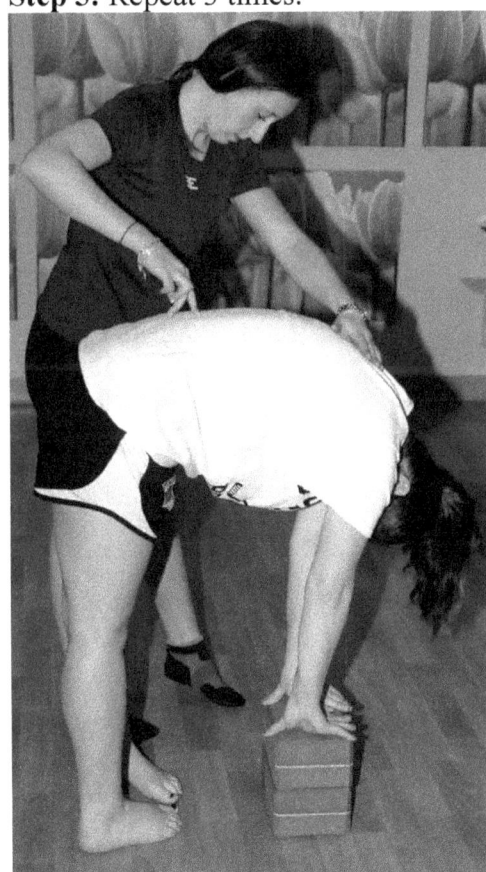
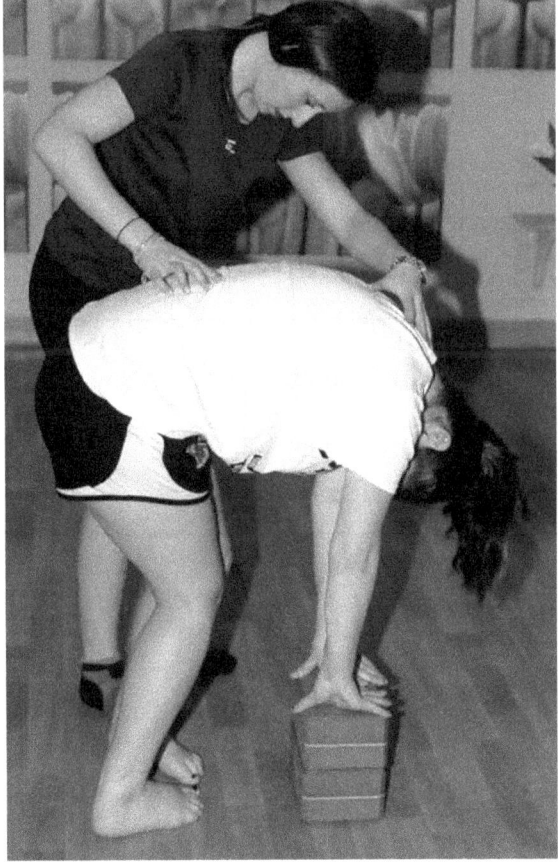

# SKATING FLAW

|  | Rounded Shoulders | Leaning Too Far Forward | Knees too Straight | Thrust too Wide | Improve Change of Direction |
|---|---|---|---|---|---|
| **Butterflies** | √ | √ |  |  |  |
| **Pec Major Stretch** | √ |  |  |  |  |
| **Hip Rotator Stretch** |  |  |  | √ |  |
| **Hip Flexor Stretch** |  | √ |  |  |  |
| **Glute Stretch** |  |  |  | √ |  |
| **TFL Stretch** |  |  |  | √ |  |
| **Calf Stretch** |  | √ | √ |  |  |
| **Hamstring Stretch** |  | √ | √ |  |  |

(CORRECTIVE EXERCISE)

*Greatness is your destiny!*

# NUTRITION

Hockey is a demanding sport that requires quick thinking, stamina, strength, power and athleticism. A great way to get the extra edge on the ice is by eating healthy. A well balanced diet can help a player react quicker, play better and recover faster. Get the benefits of a well balanced diet by following the list of **NUTRITIONAL TIPS** below.

**TOP 4 NUTRITIONAL TIPS**

*1. Drink Water.* It is ideal to drink about one half of your bodyweight in ounces of water everyday. For example, if an athlete weighs 100 pounds, he should drink 50 ounces of water daily. Start the day off with 1-2 cups of water and stay well hydrated throughout the day. Make sure to bring plenty of *water* to practices and games. Avoid artificially flavored and colored sports drinks.

*2. Eat Breakfast.* There is an old saying that "Breakfast is the most important meal of the day." This is true because a healthy breakfast can positively affect an athlete's mood, energy and focus for a large part of the day. In order to get the best results, eat a breakfast with plenty of protein. The best protein choices include meat, poultry or fish for the main portion. Combine a protein source with nuts, low sugar fruit and/or vegetables on the side to get the best results. *Sounds like dinner, right?*

Here are a few *Breakfast* examples:

- 1 beef or bison patty, 1 handful of macadamia nuts, and an apple.
- 4-6 ounces of salmon, 1 handful of almonds, and green beans.
- 3-4 slices of organic bacon, 2 whole eggs and fresh carrots.
- 1 chicken thigh or breast, 1 handful of cashews, and a small bowl of berries.

***3. Eat real food (whole food).*** Healthy, real food choices include:

- Meat
- Poultry
- Seafood
- Eggs
- Fruits and vegetables
- Nuts and seeds
- Dairy
- Whole grains
- Oils (Olive, coconut, butter)
- Natural sweeteners (honey, maple syrup)

***4. Stay away from junk food.*** Foods to *avoid* include:

- Sports drinks, soda and fruit punch
- Fast food
- Candy
- Cookies, cakes and doughnuts
- Chips
- Artificial ingredients and flavor enhancers (MSG, colorings and sweeteners)
- Refined grains (most breads, cereals, pastas, cookies and cakes)
- Imitation foods (margarine, fake butter, soy milk)
- Products that contain corn syrup

---

*You deserve to succeed! Don't let anyone or anything hold you back!*

## PRE-GAME MEAL

A very common question that hockey players ask is "What should I eat on game day?" Unfortunately, the answer to this question is not so simple. This is because a meal that may work well for one athlete is not always guaranteed to work well for another. Finding the best pre-game meal requires some experimenting. Use skills sessions and practices to experiment with different food combinations. For best results follow the rules listed within the **TOP 4 NUTRITIONAL TIPS** and the **PRE-GAME SUGGESTIONS** below.

## TOP 4 NUTRITIONAL TIPS

- Drink water
- Eat Breakfast
- Eat real food
- Avoid junk food

## PRE-GAME SUGGESTIONS

- Avoid sugary foods, sports drinks and juices.
- Avoid dairy
- Avoid spicy foods
- Eat a pre-game meal 30-45 minutes before warm-ups. Choose from the **Breakfast examples.**
- Choose *low sugar fruit* before games (berries, oranges, apples, pears, coconut)
- Avoid *high sugar fruit* before games (bananas, grapes, pineapple, melon)

---

*Motivate yourself! Don't wait for someone else to do it!*

*Barbara Williams with her students and Dawn Sikorski at Institute 3E Gym, Huntington, NY*

# CHAPTER 3
## EVERYTHING YOU WANTED TO KNOW ABOUT SKATES

*Robert from Port Jeff Sports (Port Jeff Station, NY) sizes a player*

***Skates*** – After you get your body in shape, it is time to purchase a good pair of skates. Many people don't realize that the skate is the most important piece of equipment that must be purchased from either a pro shop inside the ice rink, or a sports store that specializes in selling hockey skates. You have to be fitted wearing nylon socks, not thick socks, and it has to fit like a glove, which means 1 1/2 sizes smaller than your normal shoe size.

*Remember, you've got what it takes!*

Many parents buy skates for their children the same size as their shoe size, or larger. The parents figure the child will get a lot more use out of the skates and also save them money. This is untrue. The better the fit, the better the skate enables you to execute all of the power skating techniques. Remember, if you are a young serious skater, you will have to commit yourself to buying a new pair of skates every year. I have even seen a few children purchase two pairs of skates a season because of their growth spurt. Remember, if you invest in cheap skates, the skate boot will break down faster, and a cheaper quality blade will not hold a good sharpening.

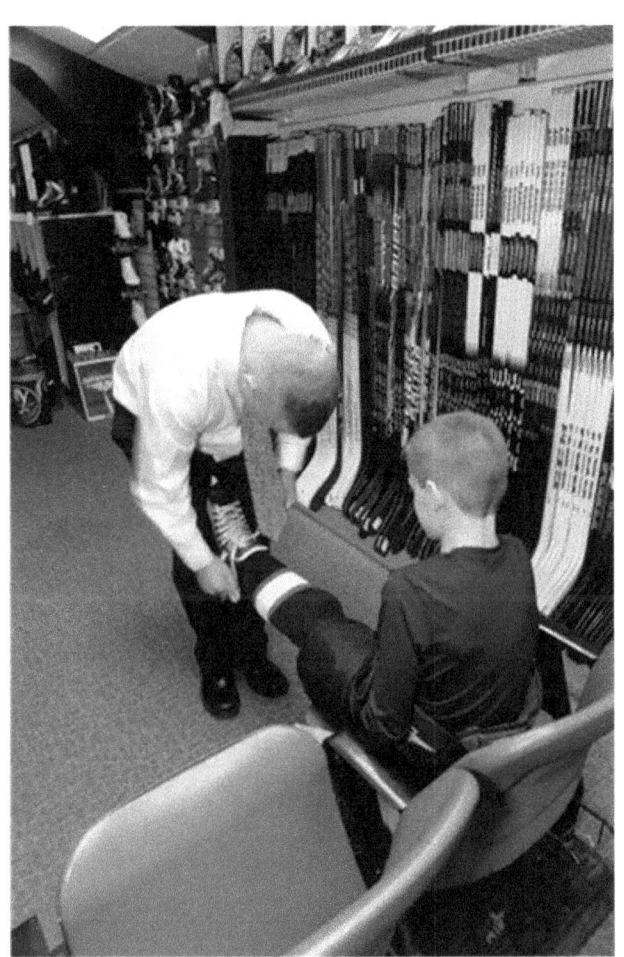

It is wiser from the start to spend the extra money on a good quality skate. It will save you a lot of grief later on. Also, forget "trade in" or "swap" skates unless you are just going to skate once in a while during a public session or on a pond. If you are a serious skater or going to skate on a team, you need to purchase good quality skates. After you purchase your skates, remember that every third or fourth time skating on them, they must be sharpened. Also, when you are purchasing your skates, ask the salesman to show you how to lace up your boot. Lacing up your skate the correct way will give you 100% support on the ice.

---

*Fill your mind and body with positive thoughts!*

Many parents lace their children's skates too tightly causing poor circulation, foot cramps and even pain. Below is a diagram of how your skates should be properly laced. It is a good idea to purchase a skate hook to tighten your skates, and also get some terry cloth skate guards to protect the blades while they are in your bag. If your parents are dropping you off at the front door of the rink and you are getting out of the car fully dressed with your skates on, then you need to purchase plastic skate guards. I have only seen this happen on a recreational level. I don't recommend this method, it is better to put your skates on inside of the rink. Always make sure you purchase two pairs of skate laces for your skates because laces have a habit of breaking in the middle of a game, so always be prepared. You should carry a few terrycloth rags to dry your skates off after a game because the blades will rust if you don't.

**Understanding the construction of the skate blade will help parents as well as the hockey player understand how to skate properly. (See Illustration Below)**

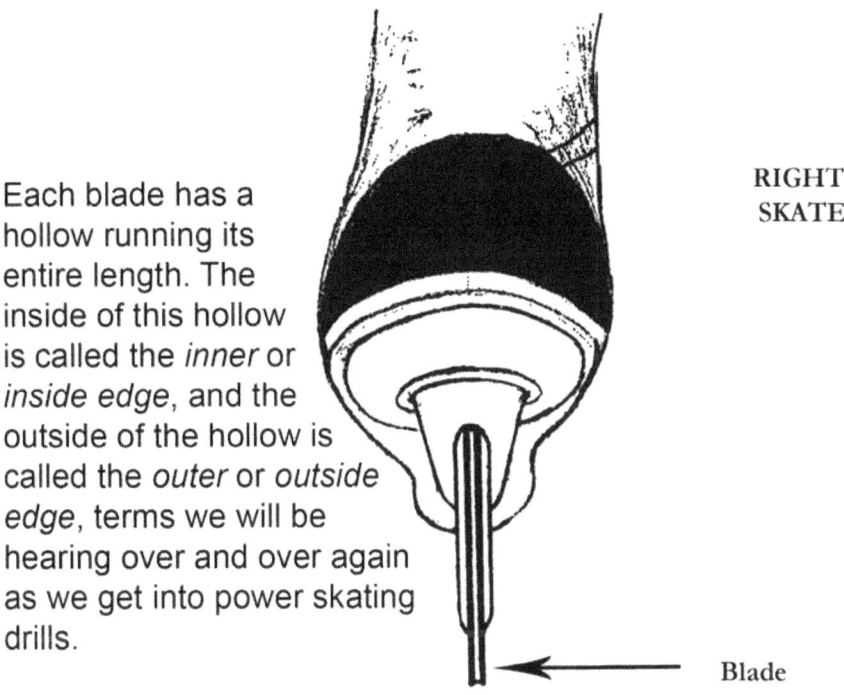

Each blade has a hollow running its entire length. The inside of this hollow is called the *inner* or *inside edge*, and the outside of the hollow is called the *outer* or *outside edge*, terms we will be hearing over and over again as we get into power skating drills.

RIGHT SKATE

Blade

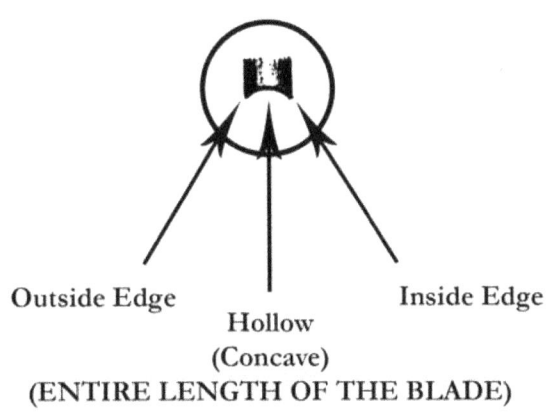

Outside Edge     Inside Edge
Hollow
(Concave)
(ENTIRE LENGTH OF THE BLADE)

**Understanding about the flats, inside and outside edges of your skates will be beneficial in understanding how to properly power skate. (See Illustration Below)**

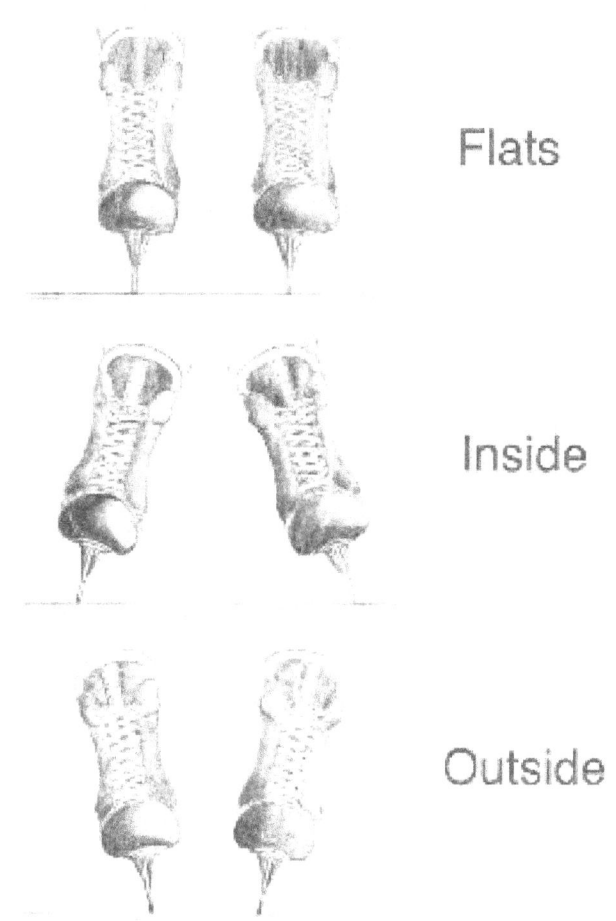

Most children get their skates sharpened every third or fourth time that they skate. For the more serious player that plays on a travel team, profiling your skates is the way to go, all the way from a mite up to an NHL Player.

The cost of "travel hockey" is very expensive. Good skates, equipment, registration and traveling to and from hotels are just some of the expenses incurred. Skate maintenance is overlooked because of not understanding the importance of how the skate works with the skater. A properly profiled skate blade means the two blades have the same shape, blade heights, pitch and alignment, which works for the skaters' favor and not against them. Bob Allen, who developed "Maximum Edge," prides himself with his proven skate maintenance system. Bob feels coaches and parents cannot ask their skaters to perform at 100% when their skate sharpening is performing at 60%. If your home rink does not have a person that profiles skates, you can get in touch with Bob Allen at maxedge@mnsi.net

Now that we have purchased our skates and understand how the skates function, we are now ready to purchase the rest of our equipment.

*You have the "power" to make great things happen for yourself!*

## PROPER EQUIPMENT

After you purchase your skates, you are now ready to purchase the rest of your equipment. You will need an Under Armour shirt for your chest and a "jock short" on the bottom. Years ago, everyone would wear long underwear and a jockstrap that held the supporter cup. Nowadays the jock short has the athletic supporter cup built into it as well as the Velcro to hold your socks up. I will never forget a story concerning an athletic supporter cup. I had just started to teach older boys, (16 to 18 years old) and I was still very unfamiliar with a lot of the standard hockey equipment that was used, especially everything that they wore under the jerseys and pants. One night I was training 30 boys and we were skating down the ice at a high-speed and all of a sudden I saw something on the ice. I skated over to it and picked it up, thinking it was a piece of plastic from the player's hockey pants. I was a little upset because any object on the ice is a potential danger to the player as well as myself. All I kept thinking was that if I tripped on that I would break my neck. So in a loud voice I yelled, "Okay fellas, who owns this?"

There was complete silence, and after a moment, I repeated myself even louder. Still no response. Then one of the fathers called me over to the boards. He asked me in a whisper if I knew what I was holding. I muttered something about plastic that goes in the side of the pants, or an elbow, or knee protector. Quietly he said, "Barbara, you are holding an athletic supporter cup!" I couldn't believe what I was hearing! I almost died from embarrassment. The heat from my red face almost melted the ice under me as I stood there holding the athletic support cup! Suddenly there was a loud outburst of laughter from all 30 boys, as well as the fathers in the stands. I could hardly look at the boys faces, although I must admit I started to chuckle myself. I just said in a loud voice, "Boys take a few minutes, go into the locker room and find out who owns this lost piece of equipment." Needless to say I heard the laughter get worse in the locker room. From that moment on, I studied every piece of equipment that an ice hockey player wears and that was my unforgettable episode with an athletic supporter cup!

Another funny story concerning an athletic supporter cup was when my college team left me beautifully wrapped presents for Christmas. I thought this was so thoughtful. I started to open the presents, which included "old spice on a rope" followed by a Mennan after shave lotion, and a striped men's tie. Also no woman's Christmas would be complete without a pink jockstrap with a big bow on it! I didn't know whether to laugh or cry. Needless to say my next power skating session with this team, I made them crawl off the ice!!

***Shin Pads*** – Shin pads have to be fitted to the bottom of the ankle and must go over the kneecap. They also have adjustable Velcro straps to make it a secure fit to ensure protection. They help protect against injuries to the leg that the puck and stick can cause.

***Shoulder Pads*** – Shoulder pads have to be fitted to the shoulder and the protective caps are on top of the shoulder. Make sure the pads are not too big. If the collarbone is exposed they are too big. The pads have Velcro with adjustable straps and must fit snugly to protect the player's chest, shoulders and collarbone. If your shoulder pads are too small they will be tight around the neck.

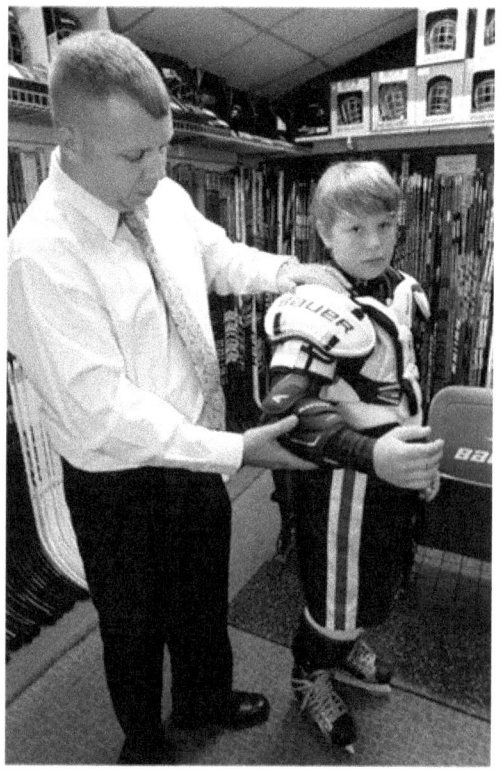

***Elbow Pads*** – Elbow pads are used to protect the elbows. Hold your arms straight out. If the elbow pads slide down, they are too big. They have Velcro straps to hold the elbow pad snugly in place. A lot of boys at higher levels have a small gap between the elbow pads and their gloves because it gives them more flexibility.

*Hockey Gloves* – When trying on your gloves always be sure to have your fingers go to the end of the glove. Shake your gloves. If they fall off they are too big. Also, if you can pinch the fingers and there is a lot to pinch, that shows you that they are also too big.

*Helmet* – I can honestly only recommend one helmet and that is the "React Helmet" by Nike Bauer. The added head protection that is provided inside the helmet ensures the safety of the child in case of a hit or fall. I personally feel it can prevent a serious concussion. Also if you've previously had a concussion, this is the helmet to purchase.

 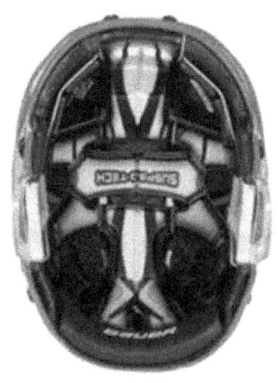

DMF's "hook and loop" system enables the wearer to pull their pant apart at the inseam using the patent-pending DMF pull-tabs, yet retains the strength needed along the inseam when the hockey pant is reassembled.

<u>DMF.com</u>

***Hockey Pants & Jersey*** – Hockey pants are big and give the needed protection to the hip, kidney and tailbone areas. They have extra padding in them and come in nylon. They should start from the bottom of the rib cage and end at the knee. Make sure you purchase a big jersey so that all this gear will fit under it because you need freedom of movement.

---

*Have a vision for your life and go after it with a vengeance!*

***Hockey Stick*** – The last piece of equipment is a hockey stick. Hockey sticks come in youth, intermediate, junior and adult sizes. It is a highly personal piece of equipment because players come in all different heights. Some players are left-handed and some are right-handed. Sticks vary for each player. A good fit for the sizing of the hockey stick is when you are standing in your skates and the stick comes up to your chin. It is wise to use black tape on the blade to camouflage the puck when shooting at a goalie. Also when your teammate is giving you a pass, he will be able to put the puck right on your blade. On the other hand white tape blends in with the ice and it would be more difficult for you to complete a pass to your teammate if he has white tape on the end of his stick. Be smart, go with black tape.

***Complete Hockey Equipment*** – Now that you understand the importance of hockey equipment go ahead and enjoy your game!

# CHAPTER 4

## POWER SKATING DRILLS

Now that you've learned how to get into shape and your skates and equipment are purchased, we are now ready to learn how to skate. In order to skate properly, you must understand how to properly use the edges of your skates. Our hockey player below (See Figure 1, 2 & 3) is standing on the flats of his blade, and then he is pictured showing his inside and outside edges.

*We all have the power to change our lives!*

Flats of the Skates

Inside Edges of Skates

Outside Edges of Skates

*Successful people graduate with high marks!*

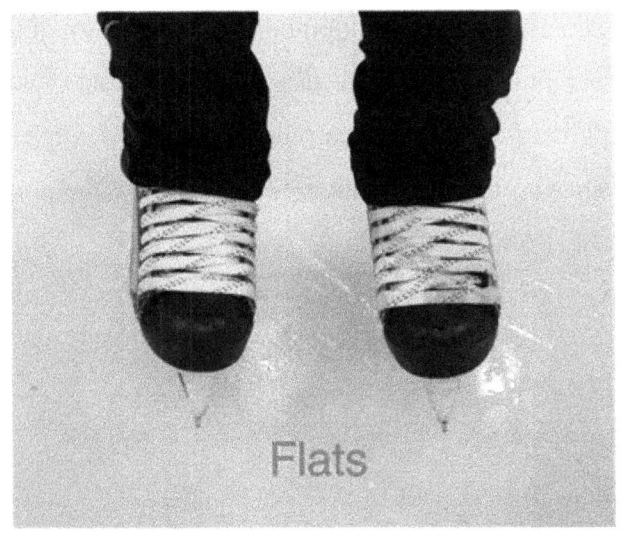

I am also showing close up pictures of the skates depicting flats, inside & outside edges. (See Figures Below.)

It is critical to your skating maneuvers to understand about the edges of your skates. Every move that you make on the ice centers around edge control. Always remember to do the following exercises slowly and correctly, and afterwards you can build up your speed. I have found that most books that try to teach and illustrate "Power Skating" are difficult to read, understand and can be quite boring. The following exercises that I will teach you in this book are easy to understand and execute.

The following exercise is the most important exercise in my book. It is called the "Long Exercise."

*(Figure # 1)* The player is standing on the ice with his skates directly under his body.

*(Figure #2)* The player is pushing off with his right inside edge which will start his movement forward.

*(Figure # 3)* The skate is lifted off the ice towards the back of his body.

*(Figure # 4)* He is starting to bring the skate back under his body.

*(Figure # 5)* He has completed bringing the skate back under his body.

\*\*\* Before you push off on your *left* foot hold it for a count of 2 \*\*\*

This exercise will teach you how to skate and transfer the weight of your skate onto the ice and ***not*** in the air. Make sure you always have your head up, chest up and knees bent for proper form. Also be sure to keep pressure on the ***ball of your foot*** and ***never your toe.***

Skating is done from your hips down. Some exercises to restrict your upper body movement are shown below in Figures # 1, # 2, and # 3.

Lock Your Arms
Fig #1

Stick Held in Back of You
Fig # 2

Stick Held in Front of You
Fig # 3

The following pictures show you the *incorrect* way to skate.

Never Skate with Your Head Down

Never Skate with Your Stick High in the Air

Never Kick Your Leg High in the Air

Too Wide　　　　Perfect　　　　Too Narrow

Proper Stance for a Player

*Welcome hard and intense practices, as well as games.
That's where champions are made.*

## INSIDE EDGE EXERCISES

Figure #1
Figure #3
Figure #2

***"2 Foot Inside Edge Exercise"*** — Start with skates under you body as pictured in Figure # 1. Push on both inside edges as shown in Figure # 2. Then return back to original position as shown in Figure # 3.

> *Do not back down from challenges.*
> *You have what it takes to meet them.*

Figure # 1

***"One Foot Inside Edge Exercise"*** — Push off on the left inside edge of your left skate… **(Figure # 1)**

Figure # 2

Pick up your left foot which will put you on your right inside edge. **(Figure # 2)**

Push off on your right foot which will place you on your left inside edge. **(Figure # 3)**

Figure # 3

Inside Edge of Skates Around Cone

# OUTSIDE EDGE EXERCISES

Figure # 1

***"Outside Edge Exercise"*** — Push off with your inside edge of your **right** skate and that will put you on your **left** outside edge. (**Figure #1**)

Figure # 2

Cross your right leg over your left skate which is on the left outside edge. (**Figure # 2**)

Figure # 3

Your left outside edge is now complete. Repeat the exercise on the opposite side. (**Figure # 3**)

Outside Edge of Skates Around the Cone

Two Foot Rink Turn

***"Two Foot Rink Turn Exercise"*** — Skate toward the cone and when parallel with the cone press your right shoulder back. Place your weight on the right outside edge while the left skate is on the left inside edge. When using this turn during a game, do not hold the position to long because it will slow you down.

*Never doubt yourself.*
*Believe in yourself!*

Block Position Around the Cone

A block position is used for blocking the other team's player and protecting the puck. Place your left shoulder and hip forward with your stick to the outside.

*Be relentless when it comes to your goals and dreams!*

Figure # 1
Figure # 4

Figure # 2

Figure # 3

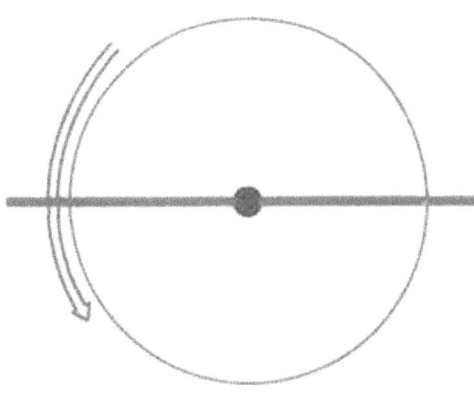

Forward Scooter

***"Forward Scooter Exercise"*** — When you are starting to skate forward in a circle it is called a scooter. Place your weight under you as you start to skate around the face-off circle as shown in **Figure # 1**. Push off on your right skate on the right inside edge as shown in **Figure # 2**, and lift your right leg slightly in the air after you push as shown in **Figure # 3.** Return your right skate to your original position as shown in **Figure # 4** and repeat the exercise around the face off circle.

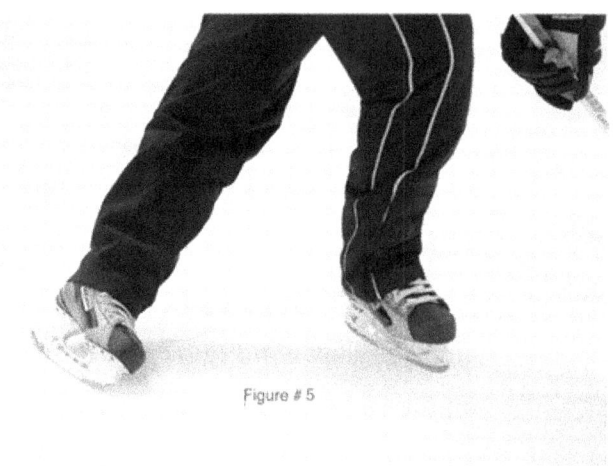

*"Forward Crossover Exercise"* — Place your weight under you on the face off circle as seen in **Figure # 1.** Push off on your right inside edge as shown in **Figure # 2.** Lift your right foot slightly in the air and cross your right skate over your left skate as shown in **Figure # 3.** Return your skate to the original position as shown in **Figure # 4.** In **Figure # 5** you can clearly see the right skate crossing over the left skate and the left skate pushing on the outside edge.

Figure # 1                           Figure # 2

***"Forward Snowplow Stop Exercise"*** — The first stop that we learn on the ice is called a "Snowplow Stop." Skate down the ice (**Figure # 1**) and press on both inside edges of your skates, pointing your skates inward to come to a stop (**Figure # 2**).

Figure # 1          Figure # 2

***"Forward One Foot Snowplow Stop Exercise"*** — Skate down the ice (**Figure # 1**) and press on your right skate on your right inside edge to come to a stop (**Figure # 2**). This exercise will prepare you to learn a "Hockey Stop."

Figure # 1    Figure # 2    Figure # 3

***"Hockey Stop Exercise"*** — Hockey players use this stop throughout their hockey game. Skate down the ice, place your right foot in front of you on the inside edge as shown in **Figure # 1.** Turn your left shoulder back and continue to bring your right inside edge forward applying pressure and keeping it parallel to your body as shown in **Figure # 2.** By applying the pressure on that right inside edge, you will come to a complete stop as shown in **Figure # 3.**

*All the NHL players had somebody believe in them!
Someone that would reassure them of their potential and dreams!*

***"Parallel Jump Take Off Exercise"*** — Place your skates under your body as shown in **Figure # 1**. Bring your right skate over your left skate as you thrust and push forward as shown in **Figure # 2** and remembering to keep your weight on the ball of your right foot as shown in **Figure # 3**. Continue in a forward jumping motion with your left skate as shown in **Figure # 4**. Once you complete the "Take Off" you are now ready for your forward stride. (**Figure # 5**)

"**Forward Jump Take Off Exercise**" — Place your skates under your body as shown in **Figure # 1**. Begin taking off forward from a standstill by planting your right skate into the ice, lifting your left skate (**Figure # 2**) and following quickly with your right skate in a running motion as shown in **Figure # 3**. The resistance exercise shown in **Figure # 4** will help with "Forward Jump Take Offs."

 Figure # 1
 Figure # 2
 Figure # 3
 Figure # 4

**"Back Skating Exercise"** — This is the first exercise that you need to learn in order to skate backwards. Place the weight under your body as seen in **Figure # 1.** Push off with both back inside edges, as shown in **Figure # 2.** Continue pushing backwards as your stance gets wider, as shown in **Figure # 3**. **Figure # 4** completes the "Back Skating Exercise."

***"Back Half Inside Edge Exercise"*** — Push off on your right back inside edge of your skate, moving backwards. When you complete bringing your foot back under your body then repeat it on the left side. (**Figures 1, 2, & 3**)

Figure # 1

Figure # 2

Figure # 3

# CHAPTER 5
## BALANCE AND AGILITY

Balance is not something that you are born with. It is a skill that can be developed. Ice hockey is different from any other sport because it is done on a slippery surface on two blades. It is a skill that takes hours and hours to master. All of the following drills may look easy but are quite difficult to perform. Good skating techniques do not only involve balance but also require speed, coordination and agility. Always remember, in ice hockey you are avoiding somebody charging at you. You must be able to move side to side quickly and effortlessly. It takes time and patience to achieve this goal. The following exercises consist of falls, rolls and jumps on a beginner's level and increase in difficulty.

***"Sliding Under a Stick Exercise"*** — You would use this in a game situation if you fall down or lose your balance and have to get up fast. Set up a stick on top of two cones. Skate down the ice at a fast pace and slide under the stick keeping your head up at all times. The skater should return to an upright position as fast as possible.

*Whatever seeds you plant in your head, only you can grow them!*

Front View     Side View

***"Shoot the Duck Exercise"*** — This balance drill looks easy but it is very difficult to perform. Skate down the ice and squat down. While you are in a squat position extend the right leg straight out, keep arms extended while holding stick and keep your balance on your left leg. Hold this position for a few seconds.

2 Legged Squat

***"2 Foot Shoot the Duck Exercise"*** — If you can not perform "Shoot the Duck" on one foot, then practice squatting down on 2 feet and hold it for a few seconds.

Figure #1

Figure #2

***"Forward Slide Roll Exercise"*** Skate rapidly down the ice, fall on your stomach, then to your side, and quickly get up. Many hockey players in a fast-moving game will slide and roll over but will have difficulty getting up because they are confused and disoriented from the shock of the slide roll. This exercise will help them learn to take this kind of shock while keeping their wits about them at the same time.

Figure #3

***"Jump Exercise"*** — Kids love jumping. Simply start by jumping over a stick and then graduate by jumping over cones. It will help you in a game situation when you have to jump over a stick, glove or another player.

***"Advance Jump Exercise"*** — The players stand in a circle and their coach stands in the middle placing his stick under the players skates. The players take turns jumping high over the stick as the coach rotates around the circle.

\*\*\* I highly recommend that the coaches wear a helmet during this drill. I did this drill while I was coaching the NY Islanders and a player accidentally brought his stick down on my head, causing me to be carried off of the ice. The following week I wore a bright red helmet and everyone, including me, had a good laugh. \*\*\*

Slalom Skate

***"Slalom Skate Exercise"*** — This is a good agility drill because you weave in and out of cones like a skier in a downhill slalom race. Keep your head up and your knees well bent with your stick held down. It teaches you not only agility but how to use your edges as well.

***"Hops Exercise"*** — The coach lines up his players facing him, and he has his players hop one foot over the other with their hips facing him. This is a good overall agility drill.

***"Squats Exercise"*** — This is a good exercise if a stick or a puck is coming at you and you have to duck fast. It is also used to elude a defenseman.

***"Circle Drill Exercise"*** — This is a fun drill. Players get into a large circle and skate in all different directions including backwards, forwards and sideways. The purpose of this drill is to teach you to keep your head up and to learn to avoid each other. Your stick has to be held down and your knees have to be well-bent.

***"Drop Rolls Exercise"*** — This exercise teaches you to get up fast in a game situation and some defensemen use it to block a shot. When doing this drill your coach should use a whistle to perform each drop to enhance faster reflexes.

"One Foot Drop Rolls

Two Foot Drop Rolls

Figure # 1

Figure # 2

Figure # 3

***"Balance on One Foot Drill"*** –This is a very difficult drill to perform. Skate down the ice with your stick held in front of you at shoulder height raising your leg in back of you as straight as possible. Hold it for a few seconds as shown in **Figure # 1.** Swing the leg to the side, always keeping your stick at shoulder height as shown in **Figure # 2.** The last part of this drill is to bring the leg in front of you and hold it for a couple of seconds as shown in **Figure # 3.** Most hockey players cannot perform this drill because of the difficulty.

Dribbling Drill

***"Dribbling Drill Exercise"*** — Up to this point I haven't once mentioned working with the puck, but I feel this is a good agility drill for the players. I have the players skate down the ice at a fast pace while they maneuver the puck with their skates. It is similar to a soccer player dribbling a ball on the field. You can use this drill during a game situation if you lose the puck and you have to kick it back onto your stick.

***"Goalie Shooting Target"*** — I like a goalie shooting target because it teaches hockey players to improve their shooting accuracy. It teaches them where the openings are in order to score against the opposing goaltender. More importantly it teaches them to keep their head up and not just shoot directly at the middle of the goalie.

***I have a funny story about a hockey net. It happened when I was teaching the NY Islanders at the Nassau Coliseum. I had the habit of pushing the nets against the boards during skating practices. This one particular day, I was skating backwards while the team was skating at me. All of a sudden, I found myself inside the net! I was in such shock that I immediately stood up and cracked my head on the crossbar. I had a lump as big as a grapefruit on top of my head.

The players started to hysterically laugh, saying the never saw a goal scored that had blonde hair and pink lipstick on! I ended up having a mild concussion for a few weeks. I eventually found out why the net was moved off of the boards. It was moved by a workman who was repairing the boards. Needless to say, after what happened to me, the players told me that the workman was so scared of me that he left the country!***

# CHAPTER 6
## WARM-UPS

Warm-ups are the exercises every skater does before a game or practice. They are an essential part of having a good game. They prepare your muscles for the sudden demand put on them by the sport.

I tell all of my players to get to a game at least 2 hours before, and stretch and do flexibility drills in the locker room. Most coaches tell you to report at least an hour before a game, but listen to me and you will have a better game.

For those players that get to the rink at the last minute and jump on the ice, you are doing a great injustice to yourself and also to your team. Ice time is very expensive, so if you can't do your warm-ups on the ice make sure you do your warm-ups for at least 45 minutes in the locker room before the game. Warm ups are also a key element in preventing injuries. Do your warm ups slowly and repeat each warm up 5 times.

***"Hamstring Stretch Exercise"*** — Skate down the ice, feet under your body and stick held over your head. Bend over holding your stick and touch your toes. Try to keep your legs as straight as possible when you bend. This will actually stretch the long hamstring muscle in the upper part of your legs.

***"Twists Exercise - Sticks in Back"*** — Place the stick across the back of your shoulders with a hand at each end of the stick while standing with your feet apart. Next, lean your body slightly forward, knees bent touching your right hand to your left foot, and then your left hand to your right foot. While doing this, press on your inside edges. This warm-up will loosen up your upper body.

***"Twists Exercise - Shoulders, Neck, and Arms"*** — As in the previous exercise, place the stick across your shoulders with a hand at each end of the stick and keep your skates shoulder width apart. Twist your shoulders while staying in an erect posture. Twist each way as far as you are able and then give an extra push at the end. When you are twisting make sure you are on your inside edges.

***"Leg Lift Exercise"*** — Hold your stick in front of you at shoulder height. Now raise your right foot to touch the stick and repeat with your left foot. Do not lower your stick while performing this exercise. This will loosen your groin, hamstring and quadriceps muscles.

***"Groin Stretch Exercise # 1"*** — Glide forward on one skate with your stick placed on the ice in front of you. Make sure the knee you are gliding on is well bent. While you are gliding, your other leg is extended behind you and your skate is on the ice. Make sure your back is arched and your head is up and looking forward. Take care to do the drill correctly since the groin muscles are easily subject to pulls and tears.

***"Groin Stretch Exercise # 2 - Sticks Over Your Head"*** — In this groin exercise your feet are under your body and the stick is raised over your head. Separate your legs shoulder width pressing on your inside edges, lean forward and touch the toes of your skate with your stick parallel to the ground. Hold this for a few seconds and return back to the original position, and then repeat.

# CHAPTER 7
## POWER SKATING FOR GOALTENDERS

*Jim Boesenberg with NHL student Keith Kinkaid of the NJ Devils*

Jim played his youth hockey on Long Island with the Jr. B "Oyster Bay Gulls" as they were called in the late 1970's. Later on Jim became an original member of the Des Moines Buccaneers of the USHL in 1980. After spending a few seasons in the minor pro leagues of the CCHL and ACHL, Jim was selected to try out for the 1984 USA Olympic Team.

Jim has coached goalies from the mites thru the pros since 1985. Many of his students have gone onto the D1 College and Junior ranks, but his greatest success to date was when his student Keith Kinkaid signed a pro contract with the New Jersey Devils of the NHL. Keith made his debut this past season (2012-13) and has a very bright future ahead of him.

Jim is the owner of All Star Goalie School, doing clinics and camps in the Tri-state area and has become one of the most successful goalie coaches in the NY area, coaching at the USA hockey national goalie camp in 2001 and being proudly inducted into the Hicksville, Long Island Hockey Hall of Fame in 2004.

Just like all of the skaters on an ice hockey team including the forwards and the defensemen, goaltenders must learn how to Power Skate too.

Believe it or not, the goaltender must be the best skater on the ice because he or she must execute numerous starts, stops and strides explosively. Goalies should practice skating drills along with the team in order to increase their stamina, balance and agility. Goalies also have to work in the crease and face off circles.

*"Barbara is a great powerskating coach. The key drills she taught me were very helpful. Powerskating for goalies is crucial for development."* –Keith Kinkade, NHL, New Jersey Devils

The game has changed immensely over the last 5 years shifting from size and toughness to speed and skill. Since the 2004-05 lockout the N.H.L. decided to strictly enforce the rules against hooking, holding and other forms of interference. Also, they legalized the long two-line pass which has opened up the game for more speed creating a much more offensive game.

*Keep your thoughts positive!*
*It will give you the power you need to have a good game!*

**Mobile Goaltending . . .**

Since the game has become much faster and more offensive minded it is even more important today for a goaltender to be quicker, explosive, and mobile in and out of the net.

Goaltenders must be able to play the puck in front of and behind the net with speed, agility and stamina. Goaltenders today have morphed into the "6th man" on the ice. They have to learn how to vocalize and communicate out loud with their defensemen and tell them, for example, if there is a "man on" or if they have time to make an outlet pass up the ice.

Goaltenders must be able to burst out of a net and take 5 or 6 explosive strides forward to get to a puck and play it. For instance, it could be an outlet pass to a defenseman, sending the puck out of the zone, or if there is too much traffic in the zone, safely send the puck into the corner while exploding back into the net after the play.

They must also be able to come out of the net and block the puck that is being sent around the boards from the opposing team. Therefore, the puck is left for the defenseman and the goalie has plenty of time to return safely to the net.

**Goaltender Mental Preparation . . .**

It is very important for goaltenders to mentally and physically prepare before every practice and game.

Goaltenders in the N.H.L. have been known to show up 3 hours before a game and sit in a room to mentally prepare themselves. This includes visually making saves, thinking of 3-5 things they want to work on mentally each game, and also physically preparing themselves by performing numerous stretching exercises.

As a goaltender you must show up early to every practice and game to work on these techniques. If you do not take practice seriously you will fail during game time situations. You must remain focused and be mentally sharp during each and every practice just as it was a game. Being a goaltender is 80% mental preparation and 20% physical preparation.

Practice mental exercises before each practice and game. Sit in a quiet place and visualize making saves, moving quick, playing the puck, communicating with your defense, keeping the correct stance, and coming out to cut down the angle against shots.

---

*During a hockey game, don't think about your mistakes. Think about how you can correct them!*

# Goaltender Stretching Exercises

An important part of the goaltenders physical preparation before every practice and game is stretching exercises. Goaltenders have to be strong, quick and extremely flexible. You should do a minimum of 5 to 6 stretches focusing on doing them correctly not quickly.

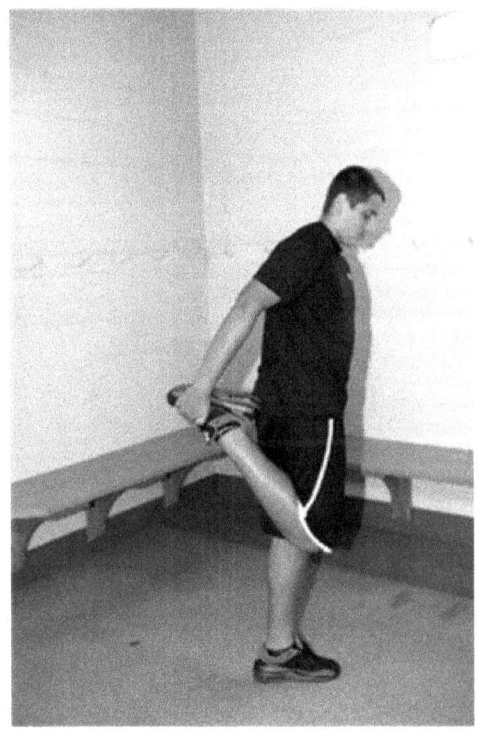

## Standing Quadriceps Stretch: "Quad Stretch"

The Quadriceps Stretch focuses on the muscles along the front of your thighs.

- Stand near a wall or a piece of sturdy exercise equipment for support.
- Grasp your ankle and gently pull your heel up and back until you feel a stretch in the front of your thigh.
- Tighten your stomach muscles to prevent your stomach from sagging outward and keep your knees close together.
- Hold for about 30 seconds.
- Switch legs and repeat.

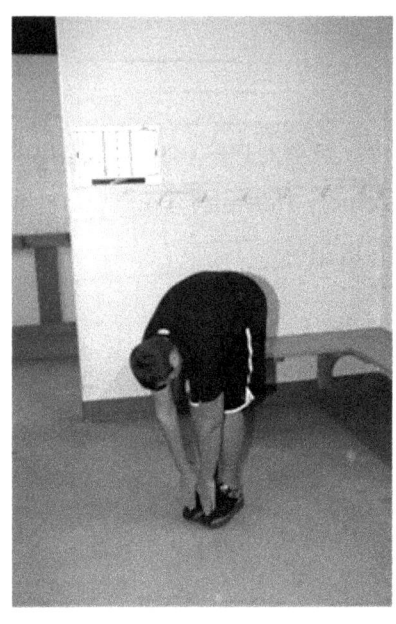

**Hamstring Stretch: "Touch Your Toes"**

The Hamstrings Stretch focuses on the muscles located along your lower back, buttocks, rear thighs and shoulders. Your Hamstring runs along buttocks down your rear thighs.

- Stand upright with your feet together, hands by your side and your shoulders lined up with your hips.
- Slowly lean forward and reach down slowly to touch the front of your toes ending up at a 90 degree angle as shown in the picture.
- Hold for about 30 seconds keeping your legs locked and exhaling.
- Return to standing position and repeat.

**Head to Knee:**
**"Lumbar Rotation Stretch"**

This Stretch will focus on the muscles of your groin, hamstrings, buttocks, lower back and hips.

- Sit in an upright position with right leg behind left leg as pictured.
- From an upright sitting position lean forehead towards outer left knee and slowly pull to feel stretch.
- Hold stretch for 30 seconds.
- Switch positions with left leg behind right leg and repeat procedure.

### Knee to Chest: "Gluteal Stretch"

The Knee to Chest Stretch focuses on the muscles of your lower back.

- Lie on your back on a firm surface with the backs of heels flat on the floor.
- Gently pull one knee as close to your chest until you feel a stretch in your lower back.
- Bring the knee as close to your chest as comfortably possible.
- Keep the opposite leg relaxed in a comfortable position, either with your knee bent or with your leg extended.
- Hold for about 30 seconds.
- Switch legs and repeat.

### Hip Flexor Stretch: "Forward Lunge"

Your hip flexors, which allow you to lift your knees and bend at the waist, are located on your upper thighs, just below your hipbones.

- Kneel on your right knee.
- Place your left foot in front of you, bending your knee and placing your left hand on your left leg for stability.
- Place your right hand on your right hip to avoid bending at the waist. Keep your back straight and abdominal muscles tight.
- Lean forward, shifting more body weight onto your front leg. You'll feel a stretch in your right thigh.
- Hold for about 30 seconds.
- Switch legs and repeat.

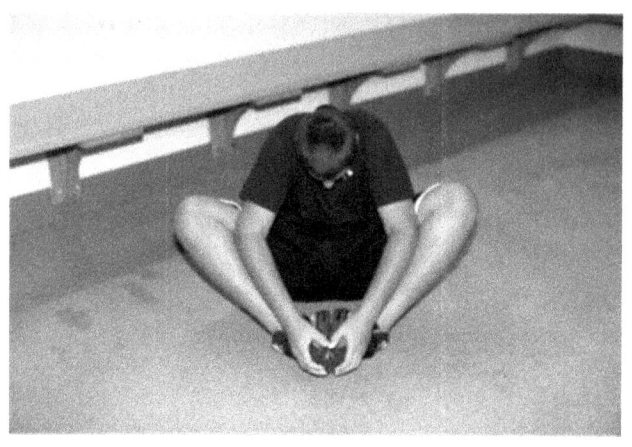

### Hip Adductor Stretch: "Groin Stretch"

This stretch puts a slightly greater emphasis on the deeper or posterior adductor muscles.

- Sitting on the floor, spine in a neutral position not flexed or slumped.
- Sit in an upright position with your knees bent, soles of your feet touching each other.
- Bring your knees downwards, towards the floor until a comfortable stretch is felt.
- Hold for 30 seconds and repeat.

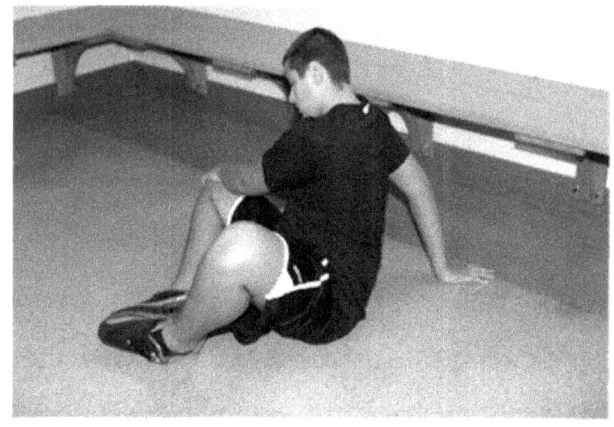

### Gluteal Twist Stretch: "Twist Stretch"

This is a simple and effective stretch for adequate hip and spinal mobility.

- Sit in an upright position with your knees bent and the soles of your feet touching each other.
- Rotate your upper torso slowly to the right reaching with your right hand until it is behind you and your left hand is touching your right knee.
- Hold for 30 seconds and resume back to facing front in original position.
- Repeat steps for left side stretch.

**Legs Up On the Wall: "V Stretch"**

This is an effective way to stretch your groin, hamstring and lower core.

- Position yourself on the floor approximately 6-8 inches from the wall.
- Place the heels of your feet on the wall in a "V" position.
- Slowly begin to spread your legs until you feel a stretch and hold.
- Gently reach up as you hold the "V" position and touch the wall with your finger tips stretching your lower core.
- Hold position for 30 seconds and repeat.

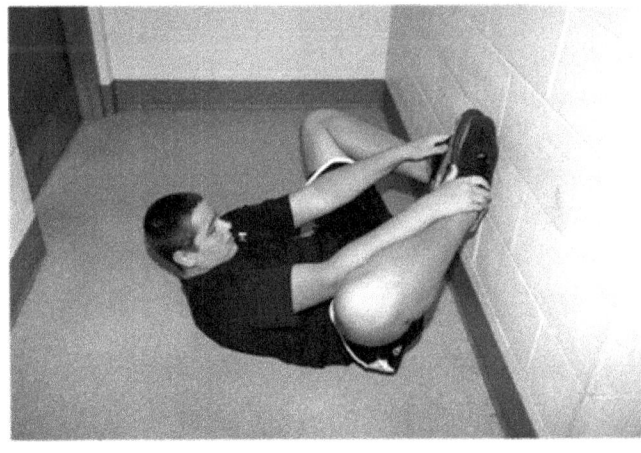

**Hip Adductor Stretch: "Laying"**

This stretch will help stretch groin and lower abdomen muscles.

- Position yourself on the floor approximately 6-8 inches from the wall.
- Bring the soles of your feet together and place them on the wall.
- Gently hold each ankle and start to lower your feet on the wall until you feel a stretch.
- As your lower your feet, tighten your abdomen and hold for 30 seconds.
- Resume in original position and repeat.

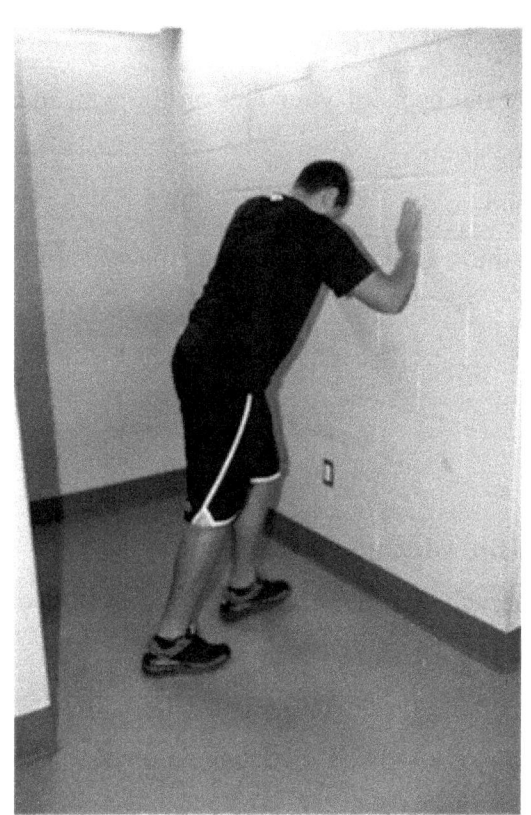

**Calf Stretch: "Gastrocnemius Stretch"**

Your calf muscle runs along the back of your lower leg.

- Stand at arm's length from a wall.
- Place your right foot behind your left foot.
- Slowly bend your left leg forward, keeping your right knee straight and your right heel on the floor.
- Hold your back straight and your hips forward. Don't rotate your feet inward or outward.
- Hold for about 30 seconds.
- Switch legs and repeat.

*Believe in yourself and you can achieve all that you want out of life!*

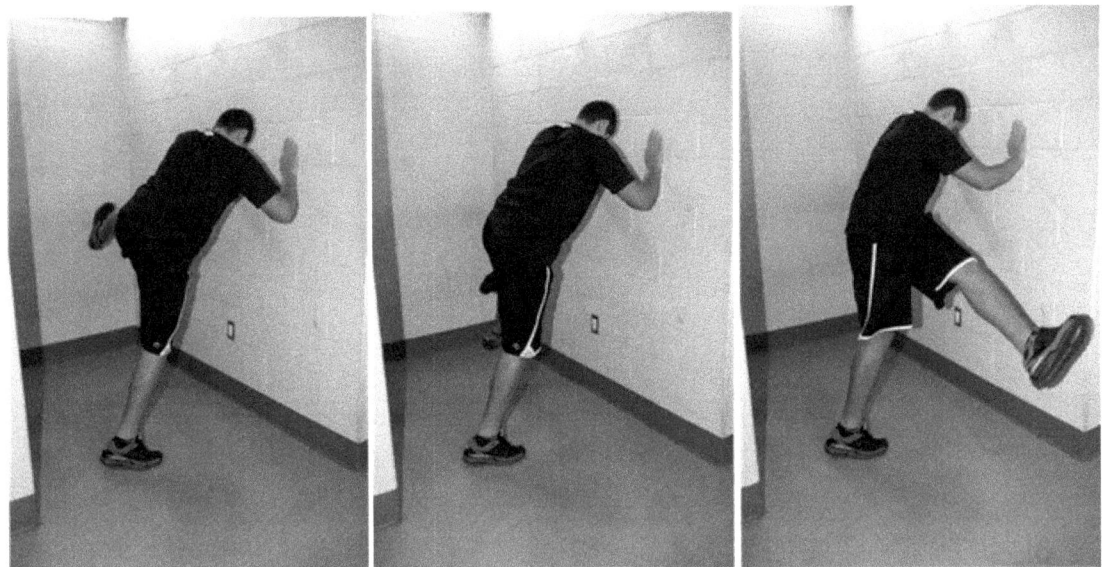

**Standing Leg Swing: "Groin Swing"**

- Standing in a neutral body position approximately 2 feet away from a wall.
- Facing the wall, lean forward and place both hands on the wall.
- While hands are on the wall, brace your right foot making sure that the tip of your foot is facing the wall.
- Slowly raise up your left foot to the left as far as you can and hold.
- Begin to swing left foot down crossing in front of your body parallel to the wall and remember as you swing left foot make sure your right foot is planted firmly.
- Swing left foot all of the way to the right as high as you can go.
- Swing back left foot back towards the left in a pendulum style swing.
- Keep repeating this motion back and forth faster and faster for 30 seconds.
- Remember to swing in an even and controlled manner.
- Repeat the above steps when you switch to your left foot planted and swing with your right foot.

**Proper Goaltender Stance and Drills . . .**

It is very important for every goalie to have the proper goaltender stance. You should be slightly crouched, pads apart, stick squarely on the ice, glove in the 2 or 3 o'clock position, and your glove and blocker slightly forward in front of your body.

    The reason why you want your glove and your blocker slightly forward is the same reason why you would come out above the crease to take away the net from the shooter. That little bit of forwardness in your glove and blocker gives the shooter the illusion that the net becomes a smaller target.

**Proper Goaltender Stance:**

Top of the crease in crouched position with shoulders squared over hips, stick on the ground out in front, glove up tucked in lightly and glove and blocker forward away from body.

**Goaltender Butterfly Position:**

Goaltender on the ice with upper torso in an upright squared position, pads are place tightly together to close "5" hole, stick in front of pads on the ice firmly, glove up tucked in lightly and glove and blocker forward away from body.

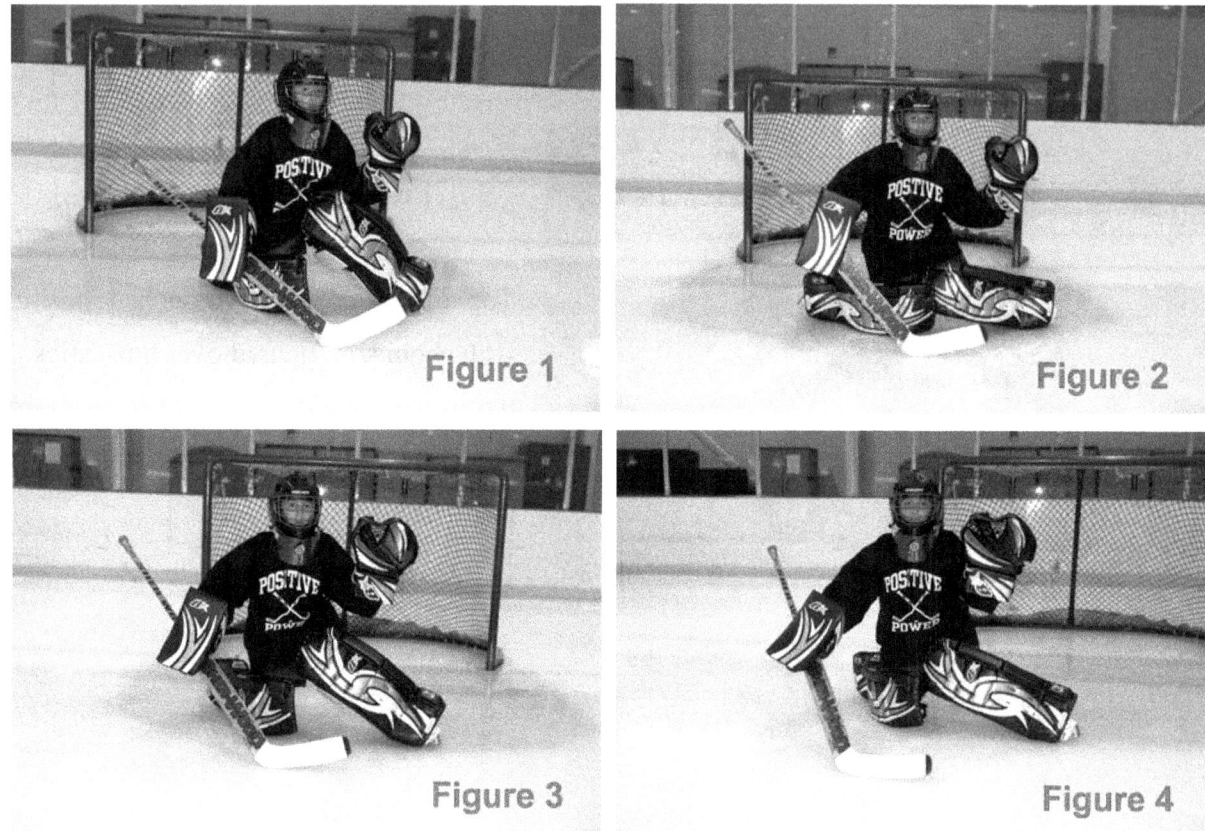

**Goalie Crawl:**

•Figure #1: In the butterfly position starting at the left side of the crease, take your left skate and place blade on the ice to begin to push your body to the right.

•As you push with your left skate you must use a strong, steady, slow push while keeping your right leg and pad square to the butterfly position on the ice.

•Figure #2: After your first full push as your body starts to stop after the slide remember to always keep your stick, glove and blocker in the same position as you originally started with.

•Figure #3: Again repeat the same motion from Figure #1 and dig your left skate into the ice. With a strong even push, push your body to the right.

•Figure #4: As you get to the end of the right crease you should end in the "Goaltender Butterfly Position" with your pads tightly together to close "5" hole, stick in front of pads on the ice firmly, glove up tucked in lightly and glove and blocker forward away from body. Repeat in the opposite direction.

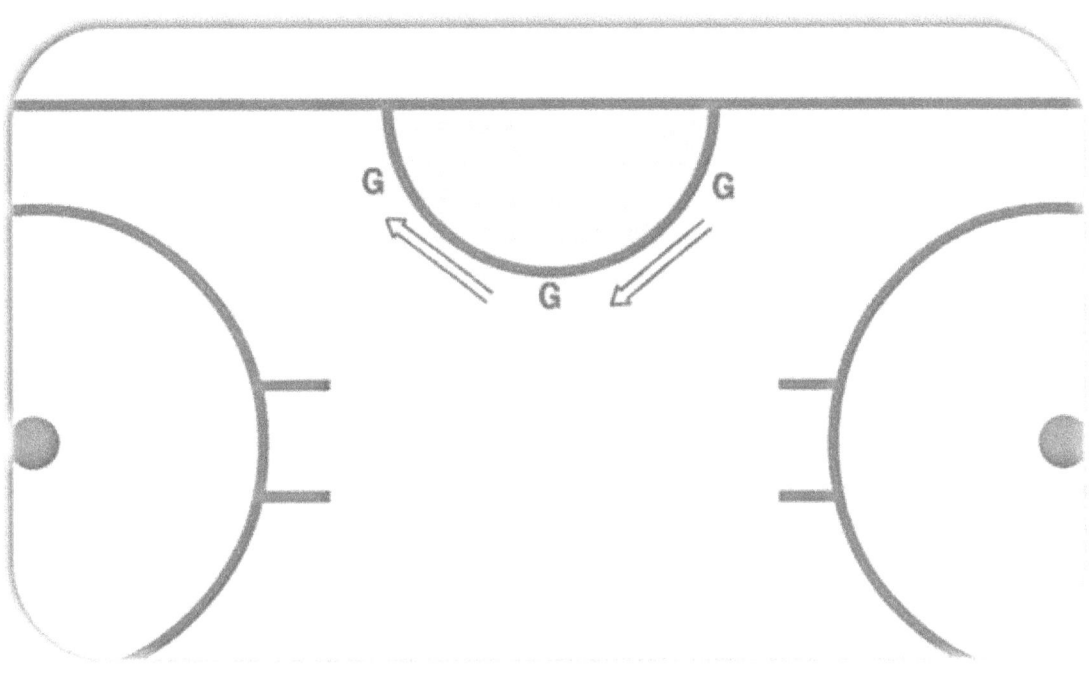

*Add determination and positive thinking to your dreams and you will succeed!*

**Goalie Shuffle:**

•Figure #1: In the standing position starting at the left post with your pads slightly spread apart, use your left skate to dig into the ice and with a strong, steady, slow push, push yourself to the right. Keep your right skate slightly on an angle, not letting it wobble, let your left skate do all of the work. The whole time you are shuffling remember to keep your stick, glove & blocker in the proper position.

*Once you replace negative thoughts with positive ones, you'll start having positive results.*

• Figure #2: Remember to perfect the motion using your left skate as the power foot and the right skate as the steady foot, slightly angled to make sliding easier. The most important thing is to do this drill slow and steady. You will become better with more and more practice. After you practice perfecting the movement slowly and correctly then you can finally start to do the drill with more speed.

• Figure #3: After you reach the right post, switch and repeat in the opposite direction using your right foot to push "power foot" and your left skate slightly angled, keeping it steady, not letting it wobble. Remember short, steady, powerful pushes, take your time!

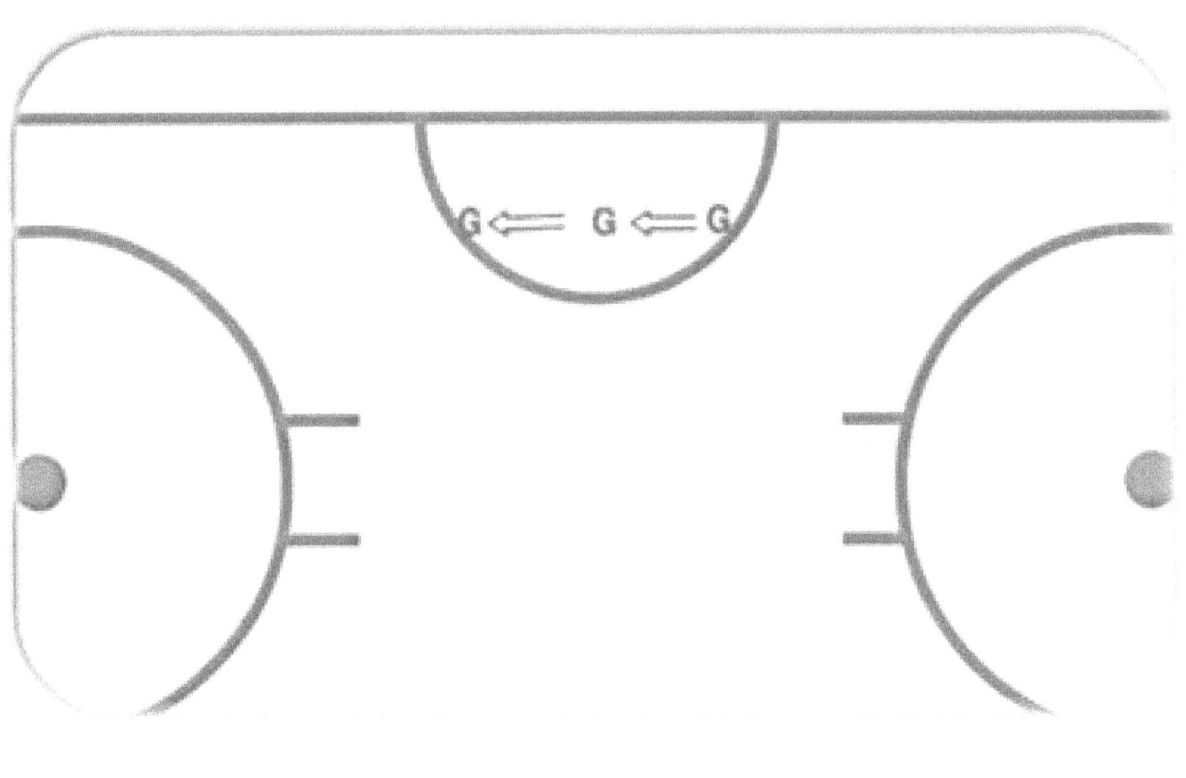

## Goalie T-Glides:

- Figure #1: Start in the same stance as the "Goalie Shuffle" starting from the left post. Remember to always keep your stick, glove & blocker in the proper position while performing all of your drills.

- Figure #2: While standing and keeping your left foot straight, turn your right foot to the right, and slide your right leg while pushing off with your left leg and glide to the right. Try to get across the crease on 1-2 T-Glides.

- Figure #3: When you get to the end of the crease, repeat in opposite direction, using your left leg pointed to the left and using your right skate to push. Remember this drill will teach you how to get across the crease.

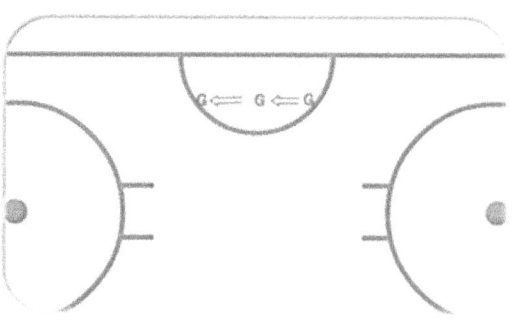

**Goalie Crease Warm-Ups:**

•Figure #1: Always warm up before a practice or a game by shuffling across the crease. Start at the left post and shuffle towards the top of the crease (Figure #2). Remember to keep your stick, glove & blocker in proper position as you shuffle.

•Figure #2: When you get to the top of the crease, continue to shuffle until you reach the right post (Figure #3). When you reach the right post, repeat in the opposite direction.

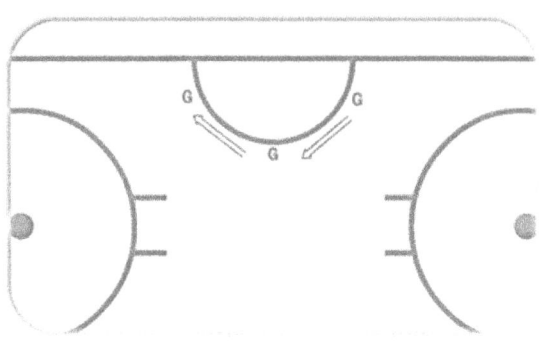

### How the goalie can make the net "Smaller."

Figure 1

**The Shrinking Net:**

•Figure #1: This is called the "Shrinking Net" or cutting down the angle. The goaltender is at the top of the crease. It is important to notice how much "open net" the shooter sees in this picture...

Figure 2

•Figure #2: Notice as the goaltender moves out of their crease further, the net gets smaller and smaller for the shooter. It is **very important** that as a goaltender you do not sit deep in the net, because the deeper in the net that you are, the bigger the net gets for the shooter. Remember to always play at the top of the crease and not deep in the net.

- Figure #2: If there is a breakaway try to come all the way out to the hash marks and as the shooter comes towards you, try not to go back too fast, remember the deeper you are in the net, the bigger the net becomes for the shooter.

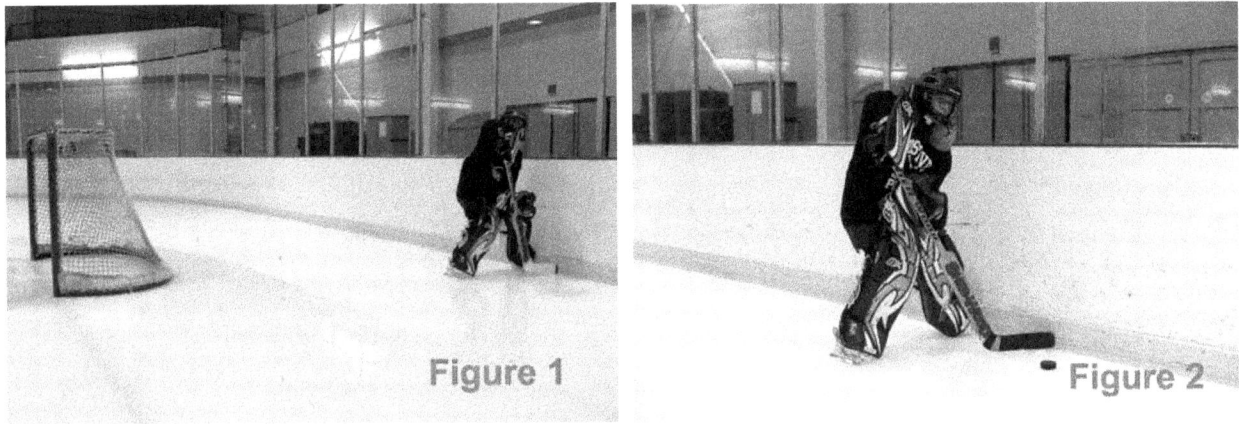

**Stopping the Puck Behind the Net:**

• Figure #1. When the opposing team sends the puck into your zone, it is your duty as a goaltender to come out of the net and stop the puck so your defensemen do not have to chase it around the boards. More importantly, after you stop the puck, you must burst back into your net. Remember, you are just stopping the puck, and your top priority is to stay in the net and keep the puck out of it!

**Playing the Puck behind the Net:**

•Figure #2. After you stop the puck behind the net sometimes you have time to make an outlet pass to your defensemen. Making this outlet pass to your defensemen will help your team breakout of the zone faster. Just remember after you make the outlet pass your priority is to get back into the net as fast as possible.

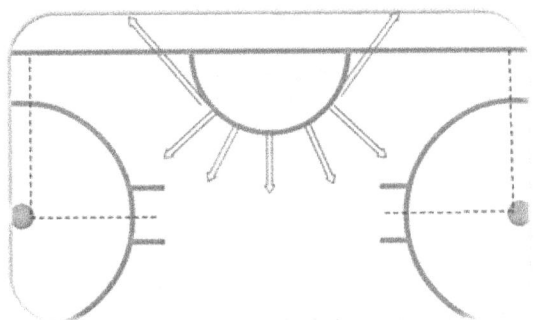

**Playing the Puck in Front of the Net:**

•Sometimes as a goaltender you might have to come out of your comfort zone and play aggressively as a "6th Defenseman." The red arrows represent where you should play the puck. When you play the puck, look for your defensemen first for an outlet pass. If no one is available for a pass try to send the puck safely out of the zone or in the corner.

Figure 1

**One Push Across the Crease T-Glide:**

•Figure #1, #2 & #3:  If you are an older Goalie you can perform the "One Push Across the Crease T-Glide" as seen in Figure #1, #2 & #3. Start at the left crease and with one strong push, angle your right foot towards the right and slide across the crease to the other post.

This movement is faster than the "Goalie Shuffle" and always remember to keep your stick, glove & blocker in the proper position at all times. When you get to the right post, repeat this in the opposite direction.

Figure 2

Figure 3

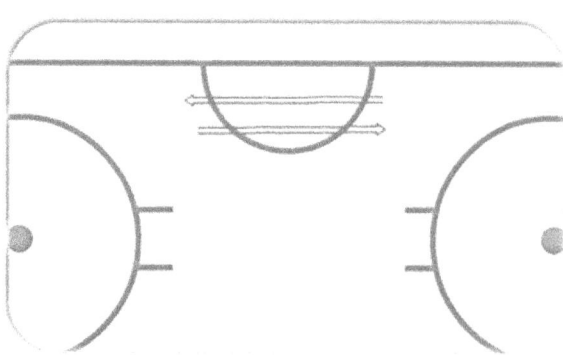

Figure 1

**Goalie Speed Puck Drill:**

•Figure #1: Place 5 pucks around the top circumference of the crease. Standing deep in the crease explode from where you are standing to the puck at the top of the crease.

Figure 2

•Figure #2: Come to a stop at the top of the crease right before the puck being careful not to touch the puck.

Figure 3

•Figure #3: When you get to the top of the crease stop and then explode backwards, back deep in the crease, and then back to your original starting point. When you get back deep in the crease explode back out to the top of the crease to the next puck in line and repeat to all of the remaining pucks. When you do this drill remember speed and quickness is very important. The reason why you are doing this drill is to mimic playing the puck as a goaltender. Just like when you play the puck in a game you have to explode out of the net, get the puck, play it and burst back into the net.

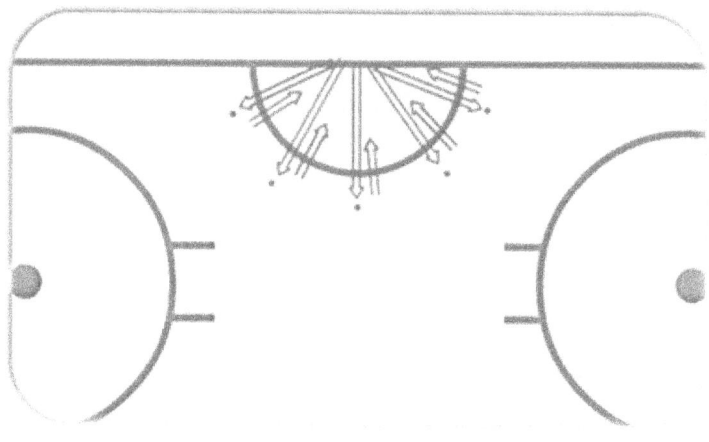

Jim instructing Nicholas on proper goaltender techniques.

*"Good communication between the coach and his player is of vital importance."*

*Always turn a negative situation into a positive situation!*

## Importance of skate sharpening . . .

Since Power Skating techniques rely heavily on using the edge of the skates and the blade edges are designed to cut into the ice, it is of the utmost importance to constantly keep your skates sharp.

Years ago goaltenders rarely sharpened their skates and most of them liked the blade very dull because they were "stand up" goaltenders.

Over the years goaltender's mechanics and fundamentals have shifted away from the "stand up" style and have instead transformed into the "hybrid / butterfly" style.

This hybrid / butterfly style of goaltending requires that your goalie skates always be sharp because you have to be quick and explosive in and out of the net. Also, you have to "crawl," which is digging your skate blade into the ice to push across in either direction of the crease while in the butterfly stance.

---

*Winners make a habit of manufacturing their own positive expectations in advance of the event.*

**Skates . . .**

Goalie skates differ from regular hockey skates. The blade is longer, wider, and flatter to provide the goalie with more stability. It is made out of carbon steel rather than stainless steel. The blade holder, which is molded to the cowling, is shorter vertically so that the goaltender is lower to the ice. The boot does not have a tendon guard, which is the piece of a regular hockey skate that extends up the back of the ankle to protect the Achilles' tendon. Finally, the boot is inside a rigid cowling to protect the foot from direct impact. The cowlings on the skates are also replaceable once the blade is rundown from skate sharpening.

# CHAPTER 8
## GIRLS HOCKEY

*Coach Olivia Nuzzo with her Lady Islanders 12U winning the GAL Championship 2011.*

The Lady Islanders are a competitive tournament-bound girls youth travel hockey organization. They are based out of Dix Hills Rink, in Dix Hills, NY. As the only girls youth travel program on Long Island, the Lady Islanders strive to grow and improve the level of girls hockey on Long Island.

The organization is currently comprised of approximately 60 players across four teams: 10U, 12U, 14U and 19U, and has experienced an increase in participation in each of the past four seasons. The program's roots derive from the former Long Island Waves hockey program, which originated in 1992.

In an effort to grow girls hockey on Long Island, the Long Island Waves joined forces with Suffolk PAL and became the Lady Islanders in a merger that was completed in 2010. Throughout the organization's history, numerous alumnae have gone on to have successful collegiate careers at the Division I, III, and club levels. The Lady Islanders continue to seek new ways to provide the premier girls hockey experience on Long Island and develop athletes for collegiate play.

The recently announced partnership with the Long Island Rebels boys youth travel program, which interestingly started first as a girls hockey program, is lauded for its potential to add viable resources to continue to build on this first class program.

Hockey players throughout time, experience a phenomenon known as *"the moment." "The moment"* is that point when we realize that we are destined to be hockey players. In that instant, we are overcome by our passion and we enter into one of sports' most tightly knit and special communities. This life-changing event has probably occurred in a similar fashion for many of us. The day probably began just as any other ordinary October day. Perhaps Mother Nature presented you with signals that hockey season was coming—maybe a fresh frost appeared on the lawn or a blanket of leaves was building up in your backyard. The anticipation of a new season would have been growing within your community. Avid fans of all ages would make hopeful claims that a new beginning would bring new outcomes. Hockey was in the air.

You would awake at dawn to the sounds of your older brother practicing his snapshot against the garage door, or if you were lucky, a homemade net in the driveway. You would watch him move gracefully around imaginary defensemen that he had created in his mind and you could not help but be a bit jealous of him. He had mentally scored a winning goal of sorts and, while his impersonation of the crowd cheering his name was ridiculous to watch, you found yourself secretly wishing the very same thing for yourself. You imagined skating end to end with the puck, feeling the cold wind against your face from your gathering speed. You would toe-drag around the best goaltender in the league and the crowd in your head would have been going wild for you too. Victory was sweet, and it was even sweeter because you were a girl! Imagine that, a young lady dazzling a crowd because she was playing hockey. You snapped back to reality when you heard your mother call your brother inside for his pre-game breakfast. There was a game that morning at the local arena. It was not just any game, but it was his first game of the season. It was a test for the local hockey club to show the community what tone they were going to set that season. You were excited, of course, but you could not help but feel disappointed as well because you were not on the team. *But why?* you wondered. Why could you not be a part of the squad too?

That was when it happened, that "*moment*." You would realize that you had woken up that morning and found yourself head over heels in love with hockey. There was a thirst that burned inside of you to be able to feel what other players felt, to do what they did. The glory of scoring a game-winner, or seeing the puck spin off of your stick to make that beautiful pass, or skating past your opponent and feeling almost weightless while moving down the wing. There was nothing you wanted more, or nowhere else you would rather be. You felt that passion deep within your core and you knew that you had to play. You desperately wanted to enter into one of the most special and unique cultures in all of sports. Your moment had finally arrived. You ran down the stairs as fast as you could carry yourself and screamed at the top of your lungs, "Daddy, Daddy, I want to play hockey!" What had begun as a seemingly ordinary morning had become the biggest, most hopeful day of your life.

For many women, this is how our hockey story began. We were little girls in the shadows of our big brothers or neighbors, fighting with our parents to let us play. We rationalized every fear they had about getting hurt or becoming bored with it. I can remember my own father, a former goaltender himself, refusing to let me strap on a set of pads of my own. It took a three month period of the silent treatment to finally get him to cave in and agree to sign me up for a house league. Nearly two decades later when I played in my last collegiate game, neither one of us have ever regretted that decision. The young women of my generation and generations prior were pioneers for our youth today. Many battles were fought so that young women could have the same opportunities on the ice as their male peers. Because of these battles, women's hockey has grown exponentially and the number of participants world wide is on the rise.

> *Surround yourself with positive, productive people of good will and decency!*

*Communication between Coach Jack Greig with his daughter Mckenzie Greig is of the utmost importance.*

As it is written in history, the first official women's ice hockey game was held in Ontario, Canada in 1892, two decades before the National Hockey League was even founded. The sport caught on quickly for women and just two years later in 1894, the first collegiate team was formed at Queen's University in Kingston, Ontario. Now, while it is exciting to know that our most beloved game of hockey has been in existence for women for over a century, sustainable interest did not spark until approximately two decades ago. In the 1990, women of all ages and in more than 30 countries took to the ice. There was a world championship sanctioned for women that year and Canada was proving its domination over the rest of the world. Canada was beginning to become a worldwide women's hockey powerhouse, but the United States was not far behind. During that year, the U.S. had approximately 5,500 registered female hockey players. By the year 2000, that number had increased to over 30,000 females of all ages. Could this jump in numbers have happened due to the United States' drive to compete with the best in the world? Or was it because we saw a different end goal--a new world stage to shine on? The anticipation for the Olympics was growing rapidly within hockey communities across the globe. Female hockey players wanted to join their male counterparts and be able to represent their countries on the ice.

Finally, in 1998, women's hockey was officially named a medal sport in the Olympics. Some would say that this was the event that gave women's hockey the push it needed to get female youth interested in our sport. Canada, having won the majority of their games in past world championships, was favored to come out on top again at the Olympic Games. The United States was predicted to finish up in second, with all other teams fighting for a seat at third, none having the caliber of talent that matched North America. That fateful day, the day that women's hockey gained the respect it deserved, the United States skated to a sold out crowd in Nagano, Japan and fought hard to finally beat their friendly Canadian rivals to a 3-1 win. Imagine that! A roster full of young, talented women who fell in love with the game and they never looked back. It was the first time a medal had been given out at the Olympics to female hockey players and the United States was fortunate enough to win the gold.

Certainly, after that momentous event, the women's hockey grew like an epidemic in this country. Little girls that grew up in the shadows of their brothers now had a valid point to make to their parents when they asked (or---in some cases, demanded) to play. The women's national team provided young ladies with the dream and hope to go along with it. Not only did the big win against Canada put women's hockey in the limelight, but it became something that was very marketable in many different areas. The media held interviews with the women's team, the team was picked to play a handful of men's teams across the country, and these Olympic gold-medalists were featured for many endorsements. Little girls were now able to turn on their TV's and see Cammi Granato, the captain of the United States, on Nike commercials with other famous athletes. These women had become our dream team and were the catalyst for the continuing rise of interest in our sport.

After the Olympic Games in 1998, many people in the sports world were tossing around the idea of the possibility of women entering the National Hockey League. The offer was made by the New York Islanders to the United States' captain, Cammi Granato, but she declined. Some felt that women would not be able to keep up with men in terms of speed and some felt that it was the no-checking rule that would sway women. Arguably, the women's game is slower to some degree. However, because of the no-checking rule the level of finesse is that much more critical to game play. The only position in the sport that this would not affect (as much) is a goaltender. In any type of game setting, the puck is the same size and the net is the same size. The speed of the shot will obviously change, and the reaction time would change depending upon that speed, but the goaltender is the least likely to feel the difference between the women's game versus the men's. Manon Rheaume, a Canadian goaltender and another great pioneer for our sport, tried out for the Tampa Bay Lightning and was then signed as a free agent. This was the first time in history that a woman had signed a professional hockey contract. She played in two exhibition games, one against St. Louis and the other against Boston, but left the NHL to sign with a minor league team for more playing time. Rheaume first signed with the Atlanta Knights of the International Hockey League and played in a regular season game, another first for women. She played in a total of 24 games by the time she retired in 1997 and has been a role model for our youth ever since. Yet one more reason a little girl can dream.

While it has been done before, playing at the professional level for women is a bit of a rarity. Another turning point for women's hockey was the growth of collegiate teams, especially those that provided athletic scholarships. After the Olympic win of 1998, the National Collegiate Athletic Association had recognized 22 women's hockey teams at the varsity level—letting school funding go towards recruiting the game's top players. Universities started to see the draw with women's hockey and found themselves bound by the equal opportunity law, better known as Title IX. Under title IX, colleges and universities had to provide opportunity for intercollegiate competition as well as team schedules that equally reflected the abilities of both men and women. In other words, if a school had a men's program, and there was interest in starting a women's program, the school needed to provide equal opportunities for both. For hockey players this meant, equal ice time, equal roster spots, equal money allotted for equipment per player, etc. Because of this, women's programs at the collegiate level were being founded at a high rate. Today, there are 86 colleges that recognize hockey as a varsity sport, 34 of them fall under Division I and 49 of them fall under Division III. This has provided a much more feasible goal for our young female hockey players, and when little girls dream of one day playing at big schools like Harvard or Wisconsin, they need to start somewhere.

In 1992, when poster girl players like Granato and Rheaume were in their prime, only 10,000 females were registered with USA Hockey. In 2010, that number had risen to over 65,500 players just in the United States alone. Organizations throughout the country are making big changes to try to accommodate young females that have found that passion for the game. In some regions, there are only teams for boys. These teams now allow for girls to join the roster and have a fair tryout based on ability, not on gender. Not all that long ago, these young ladies that tried out for boys-specific teams either got turned down completely or got a lot of heat from teammates, parents, coaches, and officials. Being a part of the minority is never easy, especially in a competitive and physical atmosphere. The battles were fought, the adversity was handled, and the rising generations are benefiting from it tenfold. Girls-specific programs are popping up all over the place and our numbers are only getting higher. Soon, the number of females registering at the youth level will be more than 10 times greater than the number of roster spots available at the collegiate level. This will make our competition at the higher levels even that much more exciting and it will create more growth at the top level--perhaps even a professional league one day. The growth of our game is a beautiful thing for the pioneers of women's hockey to be able to witness.

Every time I get to step out onto the ice to coach my team of 13 year olds, I am both exuberant and wary. I see them learn and become more confident with every practice, not just as a player, but with themselves as a whole. They are building life skills such as understanding how to be a team player, being competitive, being held accountable, having a strong work-ethic, and most importantly, how to bury yourself in a world of struggle and dig your way out. My players have developed into a family, which at times can be somewhat dysfunctional, but is still a solid unit that strives for greatness while still showing tender, loving care to one another along the way. Hockey is an emotional and powerful game. Anyone who has ever played or currently still plays it, anyone who has had that "moment" where they realize they have fallen in love with ice and can never look back, can attest to that.

I have a sense of cautiousness for my players because one day, it ends. One day these girls will play in their last collegiate game, or they will become busy with families of their own, or they will find themselves coaching years later and say, "Wow, I really miss playing." The love of the game is *that* powerful. I worry that my players will feel the heartbreak I felt when I had to hang up the skates for the last time. We all have our own story, and I am happy and honored to be a part of theirs.

My advice for the little girls who dream big, is a quote that I found taped to my locker before a big game back in college. The quote speaks to all female hockey players and unfortunately, years of research have left me empty handed with the origin. It read,

*"Do you remember why you play or has it been too long? Is it because you have worked so hard to get where you are, or because you love to be part of a team? Is it because you love the roar of the crowd, or the anxiety before you start the game? Is it because you do not want to let*

*someone else down, or do you not want to let yourself down? Is it because you love the sound of a perfect goal, or because you would rather be on the ice than anywhere else in the world? Somewhere between the athlete you have become, and the hours of practice, and the coaches who have pushed you, and the teammates who have believed in you, and the fans who cheer for you, is the little girl who shot the puck, made the save--the one who fell in love with the game and never looked back.* **Play for her.***"*

Good luck and kick some ice! (Chaper 8, Girls Hockey is written by Melissa Hauptman and Olivia Nuzzo.)

***Barbara with the power skating coaches she trained!***
***Jaime Wendt, Barbara Williams, Kimberly Lynch, and Dawn Sikorski***

# CHAPTER 9
## FLAT STANLEY PROJECT

Flat Stanley is an educational project started in 1995 by Dale Hubert, a 3rd grade school teacher in London, Ontario Canada.

In 2005, 6,500 classes from 48 countries took part in the Flat Stanley Project. Flat Stanley is a flat paper doll, and it is a way for children to communicate and get information from other parts of the country and the world. Ellie Riemenschnieder, a little girl from Florida who attends St. Marks Episcopal Academy, Cocoa Village FL, sent me the Flat Stanley doll to learn about ice hockey. I brought Flat Stanley on the ice with me and told Ellie all about ice hockey, as well as my new book, *Positive Power*. She was very excited to be in my book, and I sent her a Positive Power jersey for introducing me to Flat Stanley.

I love this project. I feel it is so educational to all children, and it was a pleasure for me to be part of it.

*Ellie Riemenschnieder*

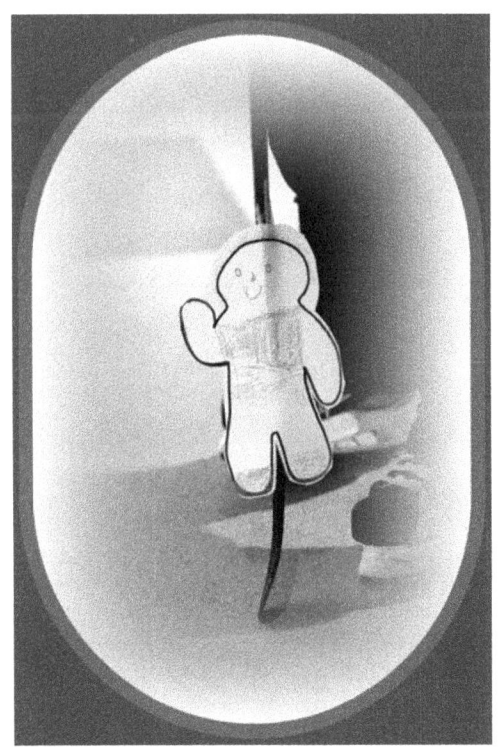
*Flat Stanley*

*Barbara Williams with her group of hockey players and coaches holding Flat Stanley*

*Your smile will give you a positive countenance that will make people feel comfortable around you.*

# CHAPTER 10
## BARBARA'S PERSONAL THOUGHTS

If you have an important tryout or game, do not think thoughts of defeat. Be positive and believe in yourself. Have faith in yourself that you will be the best that you can be. Remember, think defeat and it will surely come to you. Do not believe in defeat. That is why I have achieved so much in my life.

Surround yourself with positive friends. Have the confidence that you can handle anything that comes your way. If your coach or teammates are negative to you, do not let them bring you down. You are better than that!

At every practice and game, say to yourself, "I am getting better and stronger, and my skating is improving. My endurance is longer, and my hockey abilities are improving." Say this every day. More importantly, **mean it!** Soon you will start to see a great improvement in yourself.

I have found that kids that have low self-esteem and low abilities in hockey get into more trouble and fights on the ice. It is out of pure frustration. Coaches and parents have to watch that player and not let him fall by the wayside. Every kid is worth saving!

I want to talk about obstacles. Obstacles start in your mind. We all know the sayings *"Where there is a will, there is a way,"* and *"When the going gets tough, the tough get going."* Both are the truth. If you believe that there is no way to get over any obstacles, you won't. It's as simple as that!

Obstacles make me stronger because I try harder, and I don't give up no matter what. Walk with your head up and believe there is no obstacle that will stop you in whatever you want.

One thing that I used my whole life is a visualization technique. I tell my young students that every night before they go to bed, they should picture themselves scoring that winning goal, or stopping that player from scoring. Visualization works. Try it. With my older students, I tell them to see themselves on the team that they want to be on, see themselves wearing the team jersey and excelling in their hockey game. I have truly seen visualization techniques work with hundreds of my students. With NHL players during the Stanley Cup playoffs, they see themselves skating around holding the Stanley Cup over their heads. They tell me it works!

I asked many of my young students, as young as 7 years old "What are you going to be when you grow up?" Of course, they all tell me that they want to be hockey players, and I laugh and ask them, "What do you want to be besides hockey players? What are you going to do after being a hockey player?"

They just look at me with a blank stare. I ask them, "What is your passion? What do you like to do?"

Some boys tell me that they love animals. I respond with, "Maybe one day you will be a veterinarian."

One boy told me that he loves to go to his local firehouse and sit on the fire truck. I told him, "Maybe one day you will be a fireman and save lives." He just smiled and nodded.

There are too many children, from 7 to 17, that have no idea what they want to do with their lives. Parents should start talking to your children when they are young, so that when they grow up they will have a plan and direction in their lives. Also, high marks in school are a must! You cannot go anywhere without graduating high school and having that diploma in your hands. So all of you hockey players, keep your marks up. If you need a tutor, get one before it is too late, especially if you want to attend prep school or college.

Hockey organizations could do more when it comes to thousands of children that play hockey every weekend and nobody goes to church, the synagogue, or temple. The organizations could hand out maps and schedules to the places of worship to the parents, and if the parents want to go, it would be up to them. Children need faith, especially nowadays with the world that we live in.

The last thing I want to talk about is successful people. Successful people get knocked down all the time. The only difference between them and regular people is that they get back up and try again!

Never, ever, give up on your dreams!

---

*Be a positive role model for others.*

# CHAPTER 11

## BULLYING

Bullying is wrong, no doubt about it. It is in professional sports, the classroom, the workplace, as well as the world of ice hockey. You see it every day, and we have to all "step up to the plate" to do something about it. We have to address it and change what is going on. There is a proper way to act, and that is to respect each other with dignity and caring.

Bullying nowadays is out of control. People and athletes are taking their frustrations out on one another, with no repercussions. Many players and parents turn their back when they see an injustice. They simply don't want to get involved, especially if it involves the coach of their child's team.

Twenty years ago, I witnessed bullying. A coach would yell and scream at these young children and punish them for making a mistake in the game, but the worst of it was when he would lock the locker room door and no parents were allowed in. God knows what he was saying to these young children. I could not stand by and let this man continue to coach. I brought him up on charges, and he was banned from coaching youth hockey. I "stepped up to the plate" like all you parents should.

Just like in an airport, if you *see* something out of place, *say* something to someone. Don't ever let your kids be bullied by anyone, especially a coach or another player. Keep an eye out. Not all coaches are bad. There are thousands of coaches that are positive and make a lasting impression on their young hockey players. But all it takes is that one bad coach to give all the others a negative reputation. Please, identify this bad coach and say something before that happens, or before he negatively influences your child.

Even when I was a young figure skater and speed skater bullying was around. I was lucky that I was strong in my mind and not fragile. I never let anyone push me around physically, emotionally, or mentally. But not everyone is as strong as me. I tell my students not to let anyone push their buttons or put them down. I encourage them to be strong and remember that they are special. Building a child's self-esteem is important, especially between the ages of 5 and 13. Coaches play a big part in doing this, so remember it is important that these coaches give only constructive criticism and do not bully their players!

On a side note, a dear friend of mine, Vincent Bivona, wrote an amazing award-winning novel on bullying that is being taught in high schools and universities throughout the United States. *The Journal of Peter Rubin* can be viewed as an exciting and emotional work of fiction, or it can be viewed as an in-depth psychological study on how teens who are bullied react, consider suicide, and try to survive the horrible abuse they endure everyday at school. I personally believe that every teenager should read this book. I am very glad that more and more schools are making it part of their curriculum.

To contact Vincent or find his books on Amazon.com, please visit his website: **www.VincentBivona.com**

# CHAPTER 12

## PROFESSIONAL INSIGHTS

I have many thoughts that I wanted to share with you. Most hockey teams in the United States give a young child a hockey stick and put them on the ice when they can barely skate. I feel this is a big mistake. Hockey is a game that involves having a skill, and that skill is called *skating*. Teach a child to skate first and then give him a stick. I will guarantee he will have a much better game. If the coach can't teach skating drills, then hire a professional skating coach to do the job.

One thing that is hard for me to understand is that most teams have more games than practices. You need practices to get better, and you need full ice, not half ice, unless you are a young mite. Better to have practices every other week on full ice than every week on half ice. You need full ice to practice your stride and acceleration. Also, I see players running into their games an hour before. I feel that you should report for a game at least one and a half to two hours before, so that you can stretch in the locker room, do flexibility drills, and warm up your muscles. You will have a much better game if you do this.

During hockey games, mites to bantam, I have seen parents and coaches totally out of control. These are children, not NHL players. If you can't yell something positive to them then BE QUIET! I have also seen fathers after a game yelling at their child about his mistakes. This is wrong. These fathers should be using corrective criticism instead. It works every time! Any psychiatrist will tell you that the formative years are between 6 and 13 years old. Children are like sponges—they never forget what is said and done to them. It will stay with them into adolescence and then adulthood. Remember, these children are tomorrow's adults. Also, a child's self-esteem can be greatly affected by negative attitudes. Parents, if a coach is negative to your child, speak up, even if it means pulling your child off a travel team. Children are such a joy to work with. I observe that when something is enjoyable and fun, children will excel in it. During my practices there would be some fun drills for the mites and squirts. And for the pee-wee and bantam I would have drills that were challenging and skilled. It only helped them. Too much pressure and stress all the time *does not work*.

I love the coaches that coach effectively. I'm talking about the coaches that have nothing but praise for their team when it wins and who show videos so that the players can watch their mistakes. Children learn better when they can actually see what they did wrong. I was so impressed by a coach in Omaha Nebraska named Mike Hastings, who coached the Junior A Omaha Lancers. During a game, he had a small chalkboard in his hand. When the players made a mistake, he actually showed them on the board what they did wrong. ***Wow, what a great coach!***

I want to take this time to applaud all the thousands of coaches that I have seen that are positive and give all of their time, sometimes without pay, to train these young hockey players. You coaches are such wonderful role models for these children. That is what I try to be to my students. I teach life lessons of working hard, respect, compassion, friendship, and having faith in their life. As coaches and hockey organizations, let's instill leadership, confidence, and good sportsmanship to these young players. It's our obligation.

I feel that many coaches insist that their players skate 12 months out of the year. They might mean well, but I feel in the summer months players should do other sports, which will also develop other muscles in their body and give them a much needed break from the grind of travel hockey. As far as hockey schools, one or two weeks are sufficient, especially the last week in August before the seasons starts. I like that week the most. Going to hockey schools all summer will only burn your child out, emotionally, mentally, and physically. My thoughts on using gimmicks in clinics or hockey schools, like bungee cords, parachutes, ropes, and weights are unacceptable to me. For mites and squirts, it can be a fun time, but for peewees up to juniors it is a waste of time.

I want to talk about adult hockey players, because many parents reading my book also play hockey as well. The thing adult hockey players have to be concerned about is being a *weekend warrior* or playing very late at night. You have to be fit and in shape. It's a great idea to go to a doctor and have a check-up and make sure you are given the OK to play hockey.

Some players are overweight. I suggest that these players go on a healthy diet and lose the weight before they join a team. It would also be wise to get a cardiogram to make sure that the heart is healthy to play.

One year, I trained an over-40 men's team, and I gave them a quick sermon before we skated. I told them that smoking was prohibited, along with beer, alcoholic beverages, fast food, and staying up late. At the end of my sermon, all the men looked at each other and skated right off the ice. I burst out laughing. I will always remember their faces—they were also laughing to themselves! The bottom line: get in shape and enjoy yourself playing one of the best sports in the world!

---

*A positive attitude causes a chain reaction of positive thoughts, events and outcomes. It is a catalyst and it sparks extraordinary results.*

# CHAPTER 13
## MY STUDENTS

**Andrew Fine**

I would like to attend either RPI or Cornell University. While I am there I would like to play hockey. I want to graduate and hold a degree in chemical engineering. My dream would also be to one day play in the NHL.

**Charles Sikorski**

I want to attend Darthmouth University and study to become a physical therapist and work with hockey teams. I would like to play in the NHL one day.

### Emma Dorf

Hockey has given me confidence and the discipline to work hard toward all of my goals. I would like to go to prep school. After that, I would like to play hockey at Boston College. I would like to study being a geologist or a child therapist. My dream also is to play on the women's team in the Olympics.

### Alexander Sinesi

I want to play Div 1 college hockey. After college, I want to become a successful real estate entrepreneur. I would also like to opportunity to play in the NHL.

**Ethan Gorelkin**

My childhood dream is to play Div 1 hockey in the Big Ten Conference. I have aspirations to teach, mentor and coach students at the middle school level.

**Michael O'Donohoe**

When I grow up I want to go to the United States Air Force Academy. After I graduate, I want to join the Air Force and serve my country. I would like to continue playing hockey in college. The sport has meant so much to me that I will always love hockey no matter what I do.

**Nicholas Boslet A.K.A. "The Brick"**

I aspire to go to either Notre Dame or Boston College and be their starter goal tender. I would like to study physical therapy and use it in the sports filed. I have played on the Royals travel team on Long Island, NY since 2010 as their goaltender. Hopefully one day, I will play in the NHL.

**Michael Muschitiello**

I want to attend Div 1 Boston College. I intend to study business and become a stock broker. After college, I would like to get the opportunity to play in the NHL.

### Ryan Pech

Ever since I started training with Barbara, she has encouraged me to always work hard and do my best. When she tells me about how she trained NHL players, I hope one day I can be one of her students that goes to the NHL. I aspire one day to go to medical school and become a plastic surgeon.

### Jack Pensa

My aspirations for the future are to play Division I college hockey, get a degree, and hopefully get the chance to play in the NHL.

**Samantha Deiches**

I would like to attend college and study physical education and become a fitness trainer or an athletic director. My dream is to become the first female hockey player in the NHL.

**Nate Schuman**

I hope to continue playing hockey in prep school and I want to follow that by playing Div 1 college. I aspire to become a defenseman in the NHL, and would like to one day become a sports agent.

### Robert Mastrosimone

I would like to attend Boston College and play hockey. I want to study business and one day own my own successful business. I aspire to also play in the NHL.

### Brendan Callow

I want to go to Yale University and play hockey. After college, I would like to be a CEO for a large business firm. I also aspire to play in the NHL.

### Kevin Ioveno

When I grow up I aspire to attend a Div. 1 college and be the goalie for their hockey team. I want to play in the NHL as a goalie. After the NHL, I would like to become a goaltender coach and own my own goalie hockey schools.

### Bryan Klein

I would like to attend Yale University and play hockey. I want to be an emergency room doctor. I am interested in studying the brain.

### J.P. Morrissey

I have been skating with Barbara for 5 years. She is not only my skating coach but my life coach as well—she has helped me with things that have happened in my life. I would love to play in the NHL, but if that doesn't happen, I would like to go to college. Whatever path I take, I will take many of Barbara's lessons with me, such as work hard, be honest and have faith!

### Michael Ioveno

When I grow up, I aspire to go to an Ivy League college and play Div. 1 hockey as a goaltender. In college I would like to study sports medicine and business. After college, I would like to become a physical therapist or a sports agent.

**Chris Garbe**

I aspire to play hockey at Div I Boston College. I would like to represent my country in the Olympics and then play in the NHL. After hockey, I would like to be a coach or a scout, but most of all, I want to be a good person who inspires many people, just like Coach Barbara.

## Ice Hockey Coaches

**Olivia Nuzzo**

Olivia played on the women's team as a goalie at SUNY Cortland. She was the coach of the Lady Islanders 12U and is currently practicing as a nurse. Olivia hopes to return to hockey in the near future.

### David Pensa

*David is a travel coach for the PAL League on Long Island, New York.*

I want to thank Barbara Williams for making me the skater that I was. I received a full scholarship to the University of Massachusetts -Lowell (Division 1). I then played professional hockey in the ECHL. Barbara has helped me to be the person and coach that I am today.

### Jim Boesenberg

Jim is currently a goalie coach with the New York Junior Aviators of the USPHL. Jim privately works with goalies from mites to the NHL. He is the goalie coach for Keith Kinkade of the NHL New Jersey Devils. Jim operates his own goalie schools on Long Island and New York. For more information, please visit his web page: *www.Allstargoalieschool.com*

# ACKNOWLEDGEMENTS

**To the *Four Stanley Cup Champion Coach*,** Al Arbour. Thank you for believing in me and hiring me as the First Female Skating Coach in the National Hockey League. You gave me an unbelievable career. God bless you!

**Group of Best Friends:** I love you all, and you have always been there for me: Linda Heinz, Gerrie Hotop, Lynn Lynch, Donna Capolino, Dana King, Jeanne Carr, Karen Edwards, Mary Ann Giannino, and Gloria Ivezaj.

**To My Mentor and Friend**, Brigid Fontana: Thank you for all your guidance and showing me always what path to take in life. You have had such a positive and lasting influence on me (you, too, Guy).

**To My Doctor**, Dr. Orlando Bautista, Smithtown, New York: Thank you for keeping me healthy and for always accommodating me for appointments. Thank you Donna Farge and Zennie Nanas for your consideration!

**My Book Cover**: Jack Pensa, Jamie Rapp, Charles Sikorski, and Oliver Rapp. Great job!

**J Signs**, Patchogue, Long Island, New York. Thank you so much, Jerome Morello for all the pictures that you put on the USB stick for my book and all the help and encouragement that you gave me.

**Pro Shop**—Port Jeff Sports—Port Jeff Station and Kings Park, Long Island, New York: Thank you, Robert Rochford and Bobby LoNigro for the equipment chapter and the jerseys for Positive Power.

**Equipment and Skates:** Bauer Co. Thank you for your support.

**Profiling Skates:** Thank you, Bob Allen for the material from *Maximum Edge* on profiling your skates. **MaxEdge@MNSI.net**

**Pro Shop**—Westside Skates and Sticks, Manhattan, New York. Thank you, Dave Healy for all your help and support. I really appreciate it!

**Hockey Pants:** Thank you, Dennis Flood, for making great hockey pants. You have been a great friend for a long time! www.DMF.com

**Lady Islanders Ice Hockey Team,** Dix Hills Ice Rink, Long Island, New York: Thank you 12U for your time in taking the pictures for my book. Thank you, Coach Olivia Nuzzo for your contribution on the chapter on Women's Hockey.

**Melissa Hauptman:** Thank you, Melissa, for your contribution on Girls' Hockey, and also being such a good friend all these years (even though you drove me nuts in hockey school!).

**Lady Islanders Ice Hockey Team,** Dix Hills Ice Rink, Huntington, New York, Vice President Christina Dziadul: Thank you, Chrissy, for writing the material on the Lady Islanders. Thank you for your support for my book.

**Rebels Ice Hockey Team & Lady Islanders Ice Hockey Team,** Dix Hills Ice Rink, Huntington, New York, President Rich Righi: Thank you, Rich, for everything, and all your help in promoting my clinics and summer school on the Rebel's website. Thank you also for your support in the writing of my book.

**Institute 3E Gym** in Huntington, NY, and Twin Rinks in Eisenhower Park, East Meadow, NY: Thank you, Jon DeFlorio and Jessica Raddock for all of your hard work. You are both extremely talented and my players enjoyed the experience and your gym.

**J Signs,** Patchogue, Long Island, New York: Thank you, Jeff Barone for the most amazing New York Islander picture of me for the first page of my book.

**Cactus Beauty Salon,** Smithtown, New York: Thank you, Louis Coluccio for over 30 years of making me a beautiful blonde! To all of my friends at Cactus: Vinny Andriano, Victor Stabile, Nick Stabile, Lynn Giordano, and Kathy DeStefano—thank you for everything!

**Director of Parks and Recreation,** Town of Huntington: Thank you, Don McKay for all your support and encouragement in writing my book.

**Town of Huntington Councilwoman** Susan Berland: Thank you, Susan, for the beautiful proclamation that you gave me at my Suffolk County Sports Hall of Fame dinner. It meant so much to me. You have been such a good friend for many years.

**Town of Huntington Supervisor** Frank Petrone, Huntington, New York: Thank you, Frank, for everything. You have always been very positive to me and a good friend.

**Dix Hills Ice Rink Manager** Matt Naples, Huntington, New York: Thank you, Matt, for all your help with the ice time and the accommodations to all of my hockey players and my photographer. Also, thank you for being very positive and encouraging to me about my book.

**Dix Hills Ice Rink Assistant Manager** Donna Gomez, Huntington, New York: Your kindness and consideration towards me abounds! Thank you for always being there for me and being a good listener! (You, too, Robert!)

**Dix Hills Ice Rink Assistant Manager** Kevin Young, Huntington, New York: Thank you, Kevin, for inspiring me to finish my book and being positive for me. You have been a good friend for a long, long time.

**Dix Hills Ice Rink Assistant Manager** Walter Edwards, Huntington, New York: Thank you, Walter, for the kindness you have shown me and all the favors that you have done for me.

**Dix Hills Ice Rink Part Time Managers,** Huntington, New York: Thank you for all the favors and for being considerate to me. I truly appreciate it. Thank you, Glen Weiss, James Chang, Melisa Merlino, Joe Merlino, Patrick Phelan, Rebecca Farrell, Gina Suriano, Hannah Reinertsen, Brandon Brideau, Ashley Lombardi, Kevin Chadrjian.

**Dix Hills Ice Rink EMT Staff,** Kate Burke and Brian Hinton, Huntington, New York: Thanks for all medical advice and taking my blood pressure, especially you, Brian, when my blood pressure was 300 over 200 and you were going to put me in the hospital until we discovered the device was broken.

**Dix Hills Ice Rink Guards,** Huntington, New York: Thank you for always being my friends and doing countless favors for me: Dan Bivona, Marisa Wedlock, Christian Smith, Jordan Zauderer, Mike Johnston, Nick David, David Malglowka, and James Chiavaro.

**Dix Hills Ice Rink Professional Skating Instructors,** Huntington, New York: Thanks for your friendship all these years and your support for my book. I love you all: Tara Maceiko, Corinne Heilbrunn, Charlotte Caruso, Lee Meadows, Dan Bivona, Jaime Wendt, Dawn Sikorski, Rosemarie Coyle, Amy Rivers, Alicia Narby, Adam Leib, Linda Beach, Barbara and Lou Deluca, Kristie Lynch, Nicole Maltese, Ken Hoey, Benoit Hogue, Melinda Maidel, Melissa Levine, Andy Cozzi, Rachel Roye, and Kathy and Greg Martinelli.

**Dix Hills General Services,** Huntington, New York: Thank you for all your help with getting the ice ready, as well as the lighting, moving the nets, and putting my banners in the rink. Thank you, Jerry Riekert, Patrick Griffin, Mike "the kid" Graziano, Nick Macedonio, Will Foley, Robert Clemens, Ted Williams, Chris Thomas, Timmy McAleavey, Joe Bichko, Cory Reinard, and a special thanks to Andrea Schum for helping me with all the names in my book and for being so positive to me.

**Dix Hills General Services** Foreman Jerry Riekert, Huntington, New York: Thank you, Jerry, so much for the information about Kickstarter. I appreciate you looking out for me and being encouraging to write my book.

**Superior Ice Rink Owners** Richie and Michelle McGuigan, Kings Park, New York. Thank you for all the considerations towards me all these years and for putting my hall of fame banner up in the rink. I appreciate everything that you have ever done for me.

**Superior Ice Rink Staff,** Kings Park, New York: I cannot thank you enough for all the favors and considerations that you have done for me. You all mean a lot to me! Thank you Lynn Lynch, Kim Lynch, Mark Sambach, Dennis Flood, Liz Bilz, Pat Lever, JT Mastromonica, Joe Barbera, Scott Panet, George Eicher, Steve Rizer, Anthony Napol, Al Naparano, Justin Somerville, Roberto Losso, and Jack Greig.

**The Monfredo Family:** Thank you, Vinnie, Sally, Michael, Vincent, and Theresa, for all of your encouragement and support for me.

**Christopher Liam Gentry:** A young talented actor from New York who aspires one day to become a future Oscar winner. Chris is Barbara's student, and the way he's progressing, he could wind up playing for the New York Rangers.

**Michael J. Beirne:** A good friend that is always smiling and a fellow ice hockey skater.

**Christopher O'Hea:** Thank you so much for your support. A talented hockey player who would like to represent his country in the Olympics and one day become an NHL player with the NY Rangers.

**Lydon Family:** Michael, Michelle, and KK: A beautiful and loving family. FRIENDS FOREVER!

**O'Gara Family:** Karen and Shannon: I remember all the good times we had at the Dix Hills Ice Rink. FRIENDS FOREVER!

**Tommy Prate:** One of the most gifted and talented hockey players that I have ever trained. You could have played in the NHL. You were one of my favorite students.

**Alan Abizeid:** My adult hockey student. I really enjoy training you. You are very talented and you are always smiling.

**Chris Babieracke:** My adult hockey student. You always give 100% and try so hard!

**Miller Family:** Rob, Julie, and how could I forget my Nolan. You have worked so hard this year and improved 100%. That's because you have *the best* power skating coach. My #1 client!

**The Rowland Family:** Joseph, my dear and old friend, what great memories I have when you worked at the Dix Hills Ice Rink. And now what a beautiful wife and family you have. Lucky guy!

**Shelowitz Family:** Stephen, Andrea, Adam, and Nathan: A beautiful family. Nathan and Adam are Barbara's students. They are learning determination, hard work, and a love for the game of hockey.

**Capuano Family:** Matt, Rosanne, Nicky, JoeJoe, and Thomas: Thomas is my student and aspires to play in the NHL and be on the NY Rangers.

**Malandruccolo Family:** Augie, Maria, Augie, Marco, and Alessia: Augie is my student and aspires to play hockey in college.

**Matt Kimball and Debbie Kalinyak:** What a great couple!

**Hujber Family:** Frank, Kelly, Joe, and Nick: Nick is my hockey student who aspires to play college hockey and one day be in the NHL and play for the NY Rangers.

**Gorelkin Family:** Jason, Amy, Sara, and Ethan: "A true hockey family." Ethan is my student. He is a very determined, serious, and a positive young man.

**Mastrosimone Family:** Robert, Ginny, Robert, Nicole, and Ginger: The girls aspire to become famous dancers and dance on Broadway. Robert, I hope to see you in the NHL one day.

**Morrissey Family:** John, Aileen, and John Patrick: A beautiful, positive, and caring family. J.P., when you become an NHL player, don't forget to wire me $50,000 into my bank account.

**Schuman Family:** Carl, Patti, Isaac, John, and Nate: A beautiful family. I really enjoy training you, Nate. I hope to see you in the NHL.

**Castagna Family:** Lenny, Tara, and Luca: A loving and blessed family. Get ready, Luca, because I will be training you in two years to become a great hockey player.

**Riemenschneider Family:** Michael, Terri, and Ellie: What a beautiful family. Thank you so much for your generosity.

**Vincent:** Your generosity is very much appreciated!

**Caruso Family:** Frank, Charlotte, Courtney, and Mathew: Thank you for your friendship all these years. You are truly a great family.

**Jack Adams:** Thank you for your generosity! You have been a great help!

**Matthew Hazen:** Aspires to go to a Div 1 college, Boston College, Maine, or Vermont. He would like to play hockey while attending college. He wants to study to be a veterinarian because he loves animals and the outdoors.

**Anthony Kendric:** Thank you so much! He would like to attend the University of Notre Dame and play hockey while he is there. He would like to one day play with the NY Islanders. He also would love to be a helicopter pilot.

**Chris Goodrich and David Ramirez:** Thank you for being in the photo that I treasure the most!

**Randy Giresi and Janet Pugh:** Congratulations on your engagement! God has truly blessed your relationship! Have a happy life together!

**Ewald Family:** Dawn, Chuck, Charles, Christopher, and Collin. Keep working hard, Collin, and I am sure I will see you one day with your favorite team, The Detroit Red Wings, and I will come and see you play!

**Rocco D. Laudadio:** Thank you so much, Rocco, for all your help with the editing and making the pictures larger! I really appreciated your time. All I have to say to you is, "Rotator hip exercise!!!"

**The Printery, Smithtown, NY:** Thank you, Kathie Gabriel and Ronnie Delgandio, for all the flyers, brochures, and letters. I know when you see me coming through that front door, you want to run out the back!

**The Naples family, Matt, Jenine, Mattie, Alessandra, and Tessa:** God has truly blessed all of you with happiness and good health.

**Tom and Cyndee DeGuissippee:** Wishing you much happiness and love and most of all good health.

**CRK Electrical Contractors, Kings Park, NY, Bob (the owner):** A good and kind man. If you need commercial electrical work, this is the company to call.

**Van Cott Setters, Inc. Kings Park, NY:** If you need "a stone for your final resting place" this is the company to call. Keith, Ronnie, and Mike, thank you.

**Steven Schappert Landscape Design, Kings Park, NY:** The best Landscapers around.

**Kimberly Esposito and Mark Grabowski:** What a great couple! I wish you much love and happiness.

**Frank and Christina Capolino, and little Nico Capolino, as well as Isabel Brady and Callianna Brady.** What a blessed family.

**Jeremiah Duran:** Thank you for all your legal advice. You have been a great friend for a long time.

**Evelyn Eustace and Sharon Stark:** My two good friends and mutual cat lovers.

**Mike Ciccone and Justine Graham:** Much love and happiness.

**Rosemary Fine and Kevin Young:** What a terrific couple! I wish you a happy and loving future!

**Craig Kahinyak and Cera Kremku:** I wish you much love and success in the future!

# POSITIVE POWER

## A piece of clothing that will empower you!

Knit Hat

Ice Hockey Jersey

Baseball Hat

Crew Neck Sweatshirt

Hoodie Sweatshirt

T-Shirt

```
Sizes:  Youth: Large
        Adult: Sm-XXL
```

Visit
www.BWilliamsPowerskating.com
to order

Do not go where the path may lead,
go instead where there is no path and leave a trail!


—Ralph Waldo Emerson

www.ingramcontent.com/pod-product-compliance
Lightning Source LLC
Chambersburg PA
CBHW062129160426
43191CB00013B/2248